Reflections on Lee

Also by the author:

Louisiana Sugar Plantations During the American Civil War
The Confederacy
Albert Sidney Johnston: Soldier of Three Republics
A History of the South (coauthor)
The Improbable Era: The South Since World War II
An American Iliad: The Story of the Civil War

Reflections on Lee

A Historian's Assessment

Charles P. Roland

STACKPOLE
BOOKS

Published by
STACKPOLE BOOKS
5067 Ritter Road
Mechanicsburg, PA 17055

Photo on page vi courtesy of the Museum of the Confederacy; photos on pages viii, 26, and 120 courtesy of Civil War Times Illustrated; *and photo on page 82 from the Library of Congress.*

Printed in the United States of America

10 9 8 7 6 5 4 3 2 1

First edition

Library of Congress Cataloging-in-Publication Data

Roland, Charles Pierce, 1918-
    Reflections on Lee : a historian's assessment / Charles P. Roland.
  – 1st ed.
        p.   cm.
    Includes bibliographical references and index.
    ISBN 0-8117-0719-9
    1. Lee, Robert E. (Robert Edward), 1807-1870. 2. Generals—
Confederate States of America—Biography. 3. Generals —
United States—Biography. 4. Confederate States of America. Army—
Biography. I. Title.
E467.1.L4RR65   1995
973.73′092—dc20
    [B]   95-3685
                                                                      CIP

To Gloria and Otis A. Singletary

"Him You Set on a High Column"

Contents

Lee at Thirty-one: "The Handsomest Man in the Army"

Acknowledgments

I wish to express my gratitude to Gary W. Gallagher, T. Michael Parrish, and V. Jacque Voegeli for their kindness in reading an early form of the manuscript of this book and for their invaluable suggestions for improving it. I am indebted to Thomas H. Appleton, Jr., for his expert assistance in correcting the page proofs, and to Lynn Hiler for her careful preparation of the manuscript. My wife, Allie Lee Roland, has played her usual role as my most demanding and at the same time most encouraging critic.

Prologue

Robert E. Lee is America's great tragic hero, in the classical use of the term, doomed by a fatal flaw in one of his cardinal virtues, loyalty. He was a marvelously gifted soldier and an ardently devoted patriot, yet he defended the most unacceptable of American causes, secession and slavery, and he suffered the most un-American of experiences, defeat.

Still he rose to hold a place in the nation's pantheon of demigods. Shortly after his death an admiring southern biographer addressed Lee in apostrophe with words of pathos: "Yea, ride away, thou defeated general: Ride through the broken fragments of thy shattered army, ride through thy war-wasted land, amid thy desolate and stricken people. But know that thou art riding on Fame's highest way." These were also words of prophecy. Two of the most eminent figures of the twentieth century spoke for multitudes in paying homage to Lee. President Dwight D. Eisenhower described him as an inspiring leader of selfless dedication to duty, a man "unsullied as I read the pages of our history." Sir Winston Churchill said Lee was "one of the noblest Americans who ever lived, and one of the greatest captains known to the annals of war."

1

The main source of Lee's fame was his military career. Regarded on the eve of the Civil War as one of the most accomplished fighting men in the nation, he cast his lot with Virginia and the South when the conflict came, and led the foremost army of the Confederacy to astonishing feats on the battlefield before finally being overcome. The brilliance of his generalship was widely acclaimed in his own century; and two of the most distinguished historians of the twentieth century, Professors Samuel Eliot Morison of Harvard University and Henry Steele Commager of New York University, expressed the sentiments of countless Americans when they wrote that Lee was the one man who might have led the Union to victory in a single year had he chosen to fight for her.

Lee emerged from the war idolized as a soldier by his own people and profoundly respected by the people of the North. Had he possessed all the admirable nonmartial qualities that were also attributed to him, yet had been an obscure military man, his name would perhaps be unknown today. The renown of Lee the soldier formed the matrix for that of Lee the citizen.

But military prowess alone would not have carried Lee to the exalted position he reached in the national esteem. In addition to his generalship, he was believed to have displayed a serenity and grace that transcended the furies of the Civil War, the pride of initial victory, and the anguish of ultimate defeat. He appeared as the incarnation of the aristocratic values of the Old South yet was deemed to be free of the prejudices and provincialism customarily associated with his region. As the embodiment of both southern valor and southern virtue, he was credited with playing a leading role in the rehabilitation of the war-torn South and in the spiritual reuniting of the nation. Thus he was qualified to be a national, as well as sectional, hero.

Lee was admired by many throughout the nation during the last years of his life and the remainder of his century. The numerous eulogistic biographies of him written by southern authors during this period were favorably received everywhere. But the final "nationalization" of Lee came in the twentieth century. Perhaps the signal event in this process occurred in 1907 in Lexington, Virginia, as part of the services marking the centennial of Lee's birth. The identity of the main speaker lent an ironic but compelling significance to the occasion. He was Charles Francis Adams, Jr., who as a former brigadier general in the Union army had witnessed in combat the effects of Lee's generalship.

Adams was more than merely an erstwhile military opponent of the man he came to eulogize. He was a member of the historic Adams family of New England, which more than any other family had represented the antithesis, and ultimately the nemesis, of the Old South that had produced Lee. In the years after the Civil War, Adams turned to a study of Lee's career, which led him to admire the famed Confederate, not only as a military genius, a "very thunderbolt in war," but as an exemplary American. Adams closed his address on Lee with this quotation from the Scottish essayist and historian Thomas Carlyle: "Whom shall we consecrate and set apart as one of our sacred men? Sacred, that all men may see him, be reminded of him, and, by new example added to old perpetual precept, be taught what is real worth in man. Whom do you wish to resemble? Him you set on a high column, that all men looking at it, may be continually apprised of the duty you expect of them."

This admonition did not go unheeded. Great numbers of Americans, northerners as well as southerners, grew to regard Lee as one of their own, and tributes to the loftiness of his character and the sincerity of his patriotism came from all quarters. The scholar and later president of the United States Woodrow Wilson praised Lee as a man superior to every personal pettiness and sectional bias. A well-recognized writer of New England origin, Gamaliel Bradford, published a biography titled *Lee the American,* a rubric indicating an appraisal of the subject as a truly national figure. Poets Edgar Lee Masters and Stephen Vincent Benét saluted Lee in moving verse. Professors Morison and Commager compared Lee with George Washington in his simplicity and greatness. Lee towered in heroic sculpture overlooking Richmond, the city he had so long defended. Lee abode in spirit in the hearts of the people of the entire South and, to an extraordinary extent, of the nation.

In time, however, as perceptions of the nature of warfare, patriotism, and individual character and personality changed, perceptions of Lee changed also. Especially after World War II, certain students of military leadership began to question Lee's capacity as a general, criticizing him for an alleged narrowness of focus and ossification of mind.

For a while he continued to be almost universally viewed as one who throughout his life unswervingly followed the dictates of duty and honor, and who played a decisive part in guiding the South and the nation through the pitfalls of the aftermath of the Civil War. But in recent years a number of analysts of his career have come forth to challenge this image. Some have taken a Freudian approach to assail Lee's character at the core, speculating that he was haunted by the failures and excesses of his father, General Henry "Light Horse Harry" Lee, and concluding that Robert E. Lee was a man of fragile ego and a deep insecurity that he concealed under a mantle of composure and self-control. Others have suggested that ignoble motives underlay many of his major decisions and actions.

The life of this remarkable and controversial man deserves further evaluation.

Life before the Civil War

Robert E. Lee was born on January 19, 1807, at Stratford, the ancestral Lee mansion situated on the Potomac River in Westmoreland County in the Tidewater region of northern Virginia. He was heir through both of his parents to the best in the lineage and tradition of Virginia's planter aristocracy. His father was General Henry "Light Horse Harry" Lee, a hero of the Revolution, and among Robert's kinsmen on his father's side were two signers of the Declaration of Independence. The Lees, according to John Adams, included more men of merit that any other family in early America. Robert's mother, Ann Hill Carter Lee of Shirley Plantation on the James River, was the daughter of Charles Carter, who among the Virginia squires was perhaps second in wealth only to George Washington; her great grandfather, Robert Carter, was so rich and powerful that his acquaintances called him "King Carter."

Yet Lee was born into unhappy circumstances. His father, valiant in revolution and war, was unstable in love and peace. A man of willful passions, he was soon involved in amorous affairs with various women. After an erratic career that included three terms as governor of Virginia and one term in the United States Congress, a career riddled with indiscreet land speculation that left him bankrupt, and with an intense Federalist political bias that almost cost him his life at the hands of a Baltimore mob, the elder Lee in 1813 abandoned his wife and children and fled to the British West Indies.

Robert was six at the time of this family tragedy and was never to see his father again. But the lack of a father did not rob him of sound parental guidance, for his mother showed herself quite capable. She brought up her children in the fashion of her own people, the Carters, teaching them to revere God, to respect their fellowmen and be at ease among them, and to live within their means. A faithful and pious Episcopalian, she imparted to her son a full measure of her own quiet religious zeal. Frequent visits to Shirley Plantation to mingle with the throngs of Carter relatives developed Lee's social poise and filled him with an ineradicable sense of place and kin. His mother's strength of character and her care in the use of her remaining estate contrasted with the personal excesses and financial irresponsibilities of his father, and of Robert's elder half brother, Henry, to stamp the lessons of self-discipline and frugality deep into Robert E. Lee's soul. He was reared to be a true Virginia gentleman.

Lee's upbringing bore the impression also of one commanding figure beyond the family lines. This was George Washington. Lee's attachment for the father of his country was far more immediate than the abstract reverence for him professed by Americans at large. For it had been Lee's own father who had coined Washington's immortal eulogy, "First in war, first in peace, and first in the hearts of his countrymen." Moreover, Lee's youth was passed on ground left hallowed by Washington's presence. Born and bred within carriage distance of Mount Vernon, Lee from the age of three lived with his family in the town of Alexandria, the setting for much of Washington's everyday life, and the Lees worshipped at Christ Church, where Washington had been a communicant and vestryman. From his tender years, Lee emulated the virtues of this foremost Virginian and American. Lee's early schooling was comparable to that of most sons of the Virginia gentry. He received elementary training in a school sponsored by the Carter family at Eastern View, Virginia; he attended the Alexandria Academy, a church-sponsored institution, for three years and learned there the rudiments of the classics; and he studied for a few months in Alexandria under a gifted Quaker schoolmaster, James Hallowell, who provided him excellent training in Latin and mathematics. Although the supreme lessons of Lee's youth were learned through his association with people rather than from books, his formal precollege education was sound.

Lee was seventeen when, largely because his mother was financially unable to support him in the study of law or medicine, he made the decision that ultimately would lead him both to fame and to tragedy, the decision to enter the United States Military Academy and become a soldier. Doubtless, the memory of his father helped to turn him in this direction, for the Lee family, in its own mind, never permitted the humiliation of Light Horse Harry's later life to eclipse the glory of his earlier military career. Appointed to the academy by President James Monroe, the young Lee readily passed the entrance examinations and on June 28, 1825, stepped forward when his name was called and stood at attention while he was read into the Corps of Cadets.

An exemplary cadet, Lee learned what West Point had to teach him. He graduated second in his class and without a single demerit for misconduct or delinquency. The picture of a soldier, standing some five feet ten and one-half inches tall and built in near-perfect symmetry, he had wavy black hair, brown eyes, and even features. He was considered to be among the handsomest of the cadets.

His excellent grades and behavior combined with his striking appearance and ease of bearing to place him in high positions of responsibility in the corps. In his second year he was selected to assist the instructor in the teaching of mathematics, in which Lee excelled. At graduation he ranked at the top of the corps in artillery and tactics and stood second in his overall average. During his senior year he served as adjutant of the corps, at that time the most coveted honor open to a cadet. Upon graduating in June 1829 he was assigned, at his request, to the elite Engineer Corps.

The first seventeen years of Lee's career after graduation from West Point were largely spent in the frustrating, generally unrewarding, and often grueling work of building and repairing coastal fortifications and channeling rivers for navigation. His first assignment, as a brevet second lieutenant, was to Cockspur Island in the Savannah River, Georgia, where he labored for almost two years in the construction of Fort Pulaski to guard the mouth of the stream. Next, in the spring of 1831, he went to Old Point Comfort, Virginia, where for more than three years he was engaged in the building of the outworks and approaches to Fort Monroe.

In June 1831 Lieutenant Lee was married to Mary Anne Randolph Custis, daughter of George Washington Parke Custis, who was the grandson of Martha Custis Washington and the adopted son of George Washington. The wedding occurred at Arlington, the columned mansion overlooking the nation's capital from the Virginia side of the Potomac River, a house that retained many of the belongings of George Washington and seemed to retain his very presence as well. Thus, through Lee's marriage he became ever more strongly associated with the memory of the great American patriot, and perhaps in his own eyes Lee became Washington's living representative.

Mary Lee in her youth was slender and attractive, but not pretty. She bore Lee seven children, four daughters and three sons. Although in many ways her personality and habits differed markedly from her husband's, he being punctual and she dilatory, he neat and she careless in dress, so much so that at times he offered gentle hints aimed at improving her appearance, they remained devoted to each other throughout their marriage of almost four decades. This devotion was strong enough to survive his repeated absences in the service, some of them for years at a time. She was, however, physically frail, and the burden of childbearing and childrearing overwhelmed her. Like Lee's mother, she became an invalid before her time. Throughout much of his later life, Lee nursed her as he had nursed his mother earlier.

In the fall of 1834 Lee was ordered to Washington, D.C., where for almost three years he served as assistant to the head of the Engineer Corps, General Charles Gratiot. Then Lee received an appointment that afforded him an opportunity to demonstrate his true capacity as an engineer. He was sent to Saint Louis to superintend projects for opening the upper Mississippi River to steamboats and saving the port of Saint Louis from the river itself.

Lee found the task of opening the upper river to be relatively simple, a matter of blasting a channel through rapids. But the protection of the port of Saint Louis required the construction of a system of long dikes for diverting the current of the stream in such a fashion that it would wash away an island of silt that was being formed along the city's shore. For more than three years Lee planned and supervised this work with skill, diligence, and economy. Although prevented by want of adequate congressional appropriations from completing the job, he got enough of it done to save the port until the work could be renewed later. His responsibilities at Saint Louis gave him invaluable experience in his profession; he was promoted to captain in 1838, and he returned to Arlington the following year recognized as one of the most capable officers in the corps.

In the spring of 1841 Lee was assigned to supervise the repairs and strengthening of the fortifications guarding New York harbor. For almost five years he remained at this task, again performing his duties with exceptional competence. Near the end of this period he received two appointments that further enhanced his prestige and broadened his professional horizons: to the board of engineers for the Atlantic coastal defenses, and in the summer of 1844, to the board of examiners for the final examinations of the graduating cadets at West Point. This turned out to be an extremely fortunate experience for Lee. The chief examiner was General Winfield Scott, commanding general of the army. Here began Lee's association with the man who was to play a decisive role in the shaping of Lee's career as a soldier.

Captain Lee was still occupied with the defenses of New York when, on August 19, 1846, he received orders that put him on the direct path to fame, orders to report to Brigadier General John E. Wool in San Antonio, Texas, for service in the recently declared war with Mexico. Lee joined Wool within six weeks, and by mid-October was across the Rio Grande, riding south with the command as it made its way toward a junction with General William J. Worth's wing of General Zachary Taylor's army at Saltillo. Lee saw no combat in this assignment, but he distinguished himself in the skill with which he supervised the building of roads and bridges for Wool's rapid march, and in the boldness and persistence of his reconnaissance expeditions. He was rewarded for these efforts by being promoted to acting inspector general of the command.

In mid-January 1847, Lee received orders transferring him to the staff of General Scott, who was then at Brazos on the coast, preparing his campaign against Vera Cruz and ultimately against Mexico City. Lee reported promptly to his new assignment and found himself at once in Scott's high favor, brought into the general's "little cabinet," or personal staff, along with other outstanding young officers, including Joseph E. Johnston, P. G. T. Beauregard, George B. McClellan, and George Gordon Meade, men whose names would one day be engraved along with his own in the Civil War's scroll of leaders.

After the expedition landed below Vera Cruz on March 9, Lee accompanied Scott's reconnaissance party and participated actively in planning the siege of the city. In the battle of Vera Cruz, Lee was responsible for preparing positions for a battery of heavy naval guns and directing their shots against the walled community. He experienced his first combat when the battery opened fire on March 24 in a bombardment that continued until the city capitulated two days later. His conduct at Vera Cruz confirmed Scott's already high estimation of him and caused his name to be listed in the official report among those who were "isolated by rank or position as well as by noble services."

Lee's contributions to the campaign became even more valuable as the invading column marched inland toward Mexico City. His brilliant and daring reconnaissance of Mexican General Santa Anna's position at the Cerro Gordo mountain pass largely determined Scott's tactics in his assault of April 17–18 on this stronghold. Lee worked his way around the Mexican lines, then, after narrowly avoiding capture by lying motionless for hours behind a log while enemy soldiers milled about him, he escaped to return the following day for a more thorough investigation of the terrain and trails. He concluded that Scott's army could turn the enemy by circling his left flank to cut his communications and force him out of position. The victorious battle of Cerro Gordo was fought according to this plan.

In the engagement itself, Lee first guided the assaulting force (Twiggs's division) into place for striking the enemy line while the remainder of the American army began its march around the Mexican flank. Then he guided the spearhead of the turning force (Riley's brigade) in its movement to cut off the Mexican retreat. Lee drew the praise of every superior for his conduct in this action. General Scott wrote that he was impelled to make special mention of Lee's "indefatigable and daring" operations. Lee was brevetted major for his part in the battle.

When in early August Scott's reinforced army abandoned its

communications with the coast and resumed its advance, Lee once again became its surest reconnaissance agent. Shortly he stood with his fellow officers on the western slope of the Rio Frio mountain range and looked across the valley of Mexico upon the walls and towers of the distant capital. Ordered on August 11 to determine the nature and strength of the enemy positions in the valley, Lee reported two days later that the most direct route to the city lay along a heavily defended causeway between the two large lakes, Texcoco to the north and Chalco to the south. As Scott veered south of the lakes to avoid the fortified causeway, Lee was again at the fore, searching for the easiest approach to the objective.

The move around the lakes was accomplished without serious opposition, but the road running north behind the lakes to Mexico City was disputed at the hacienda of San Antonio by a portion of Santa Anna's reconcentrated forces. Protected on the east by a broad swamp and on the west by a fissured and seemingly impassable field of lava rock known as the Pedregal, the enemy position was formidable. Lee was dispatched with a strong escort to find a way through the Pedregal that would enable Scott to bypass San Antonio and strike directly for the Churubusco River, the last natural barrier to the city.

Again Lee's reconnaissance played a vital role in the American success. Lee found a suitable trail and rendered Herculean service in guiding the flanking columns and providing essential liaison back and forth between Scott and his subordinate commanders as the American forces turned the enemy's San Antonio position and on August 20 defeated the isolated segments of Santa Anna's army at Contreras and Churubusco. Again Lee received his general's highest tribute of praise. In Scott's narrative of these operations written after the war, he described Lee's nighttime journeys across the storm-lashed Pedregal as the "greatest feat of physical and moral courage" of the entire campaign for

Mexico City. Lee was promoted to brevet lieutenant colonel for his accomplishments in this action.

Although Lee's activities in the final engagements of the campaign, Molino del Rey (September 8) and Chapultepec (September 13), were not so spectacular as his services in the preceding battles, he nevertheless distinguished himself in every instance. His work in reconnaissance, the location of batteries, and the guiding of assault columns at Chapultepec gained him the rank of brevet colonel. He entered Mexico City on the morning of the fourteenth with the advance division (Quitman's), observed the unfurling of the United States flag over the National Palace of Mexico, and heard Scott's stirring victory address to the soldiers of his command.

When Lee returned from Mexico the following spring, he came as one of the nation's most gifted and renowned military figures. Scott would later say of him, "[American] success in Mexico was largely due to the skill, valor, and undaunted energy of Robert E. Lee. . . . [He] was the very best soldier I ever saw in the field." To an acquaintance Scott said: "I tell you, that if I were on my deathbed tomorrow, and the president of the United States should tell me that a great battle was to be fought for the liberty or slavery of the country, and asked my judgment as to the ability of a commander, I would say with my dying breath, 'Let it be Robert E. Lee!'" Scott was true to his word. Not long afterward, with the nation in crisis, he would in fact recommend Lee for the nation's top military command.

Lee's admiration for Scott was fully as strong as Scott's for him. From the National Palace in Mexico City he wrote to a friend: "Our Genl. is our great reliance. He is a great man on great occasions. Never turned from his object. Confident in his powers & resources, his judgement is as sound as his heart is bold and daring. Careful of his men, he never exposes them but for a worthy object & then gives them the advantage of every circumstance in his power. This accounts in some measure for our comparative small loss, when you consider the odds & circumstances against us."

Lee's association in combat with Scott reinforced in Lee's mind many of the cardinal principles of warfare: it demonstrated in fire and blood the advantage of audacity and the seizure of the initiative, the value of accurate reconnaissance, the tactical worth of flanking and turning maneuvers, the sometime necessity of abandoning one's line of communication, and the defensive strength of earthworks. Lee would one day apply this knowledge with devastating effectiveness. His most glaring mistakes would be made when he failed to heed some lesson he had learned while serving with Scott, especially that of being careful of the lives of his men.

After his return from the Mexican War Lee resumed the unexciting life of a peacetime engineer, and soon he was assigned to supervise the construction of Fort Carroll at the entrance of Baltimore harbor. He was still engaged in this task when in the spring of 1852 he received orders appointing him superintendent of his alma mater, the United States Military Academy.

Although Lee had little enthusiasm for the position at West Point, and even attempted to have the orders of appointment rescinded, he devoted himself conscientiously to the work once he was there. In his two and a half years as superintendent he wrought no radical changes in the academy program, but he did succeed in tightening the institution's discipline and improving its curriculum. He also made a number of necessary additions and improvements in the physical plant of the academy. During his superintendency the board of visitors recommended, and Secretary of War Jefferson Davis approved, that the academy's program of study be extended by one year, a change Lee put into effect but that was later dropped.

Perhaps his greatest problem was the behavior of his

nephew, Cadet Fitzhugh Lee, who on two occasions came near to being expelled for breaking corps regulations. Doubtless Superintendent Lee's greatest joy was the record of his eldest son, Cadet George Washington Custis Lee, who graduated at the top of the 1854 class. Robert E. Lee's duty at West Point did little to prepare him for the trial by battle that he was yet to endure, but the experience taught him much that would one day prove useful in guiding the youth of the South after the battles were over.

In the spring of 1855 Lee was appointed lieutenant colonel of the 2nd Cavalry Regiment, which, along with the 1st Cavalry Regiment, was a newly created organization for the task of guarding the western frontier against the Plains Indians. Sponsored personally by Secretary of War Jefferson Davis, these new regiments were staffed with the elite of the officer corps. This was especially true of the 2nd Cavalry, which was placed under the command of Davis's and Lee's fellow cadet and friend, Colonel Albert Sidney Johnston, who had distinguished himself in the battle of Monterrey during the Mexican War. Included among the other officers of the regiment were Majors William J. Hardee and George H. Thomas, Captains Earl Van Dorn, E. Kirby Smith, and George Stoneman, and Lieutenants John Bell Hood and Charles W. Field, men whose names would in time become famous in the annals of both armies in the Civil War.

Only after a year of frustrating duty on courts-martial here and there was Lee able to join the 2nd Cavalry on the Texas frontier. Then for the next fifteen months he lived the stern life and ate the rough fare of Camp Cooper, a lonely outpost on the Clear Fork of the Brazos River near the present site of Abilene, Texas. Placed in command of a detachment of two squadrons, he was constantly occupied in keeping the Comanche at bay until, in July 1857, he was called to San Antonio to take command of the regiment in place of Colonel Johnston, who had been assigned to lead an expedition against the Mormon insurrection in Utah

Territory. Lee remained in San Antonio until late October, when he received word of his father-in-law's death and obtained leave to return to Arlington to assist in settling the estate.

For more than two years Lee was absent from the army, wrestling with the legal problems of administering the Custis estate and the practical problems of farming the land of Arlington in a futile effort to make it pay. This involved managing the slaves, which Lee did with kindness, notwithstanding that he was obliged to have two of them who had run away arrested and brought back to him. Ultimately he emancipated all of them in compliance with his father-in-law's will.

Lee was at Arlington when on October 17, 1859, he received orders that for the first time involved him in actual defense of the soil of Virginia, orders to command a detachment of United States Marines in quelling John Brown's attempted slave rebellion at Harpers Ferry, an episode that confirmed in the southern mind the worst fears regarding the plans of the northern abolitionists. Lee accomplished his mission at Harpers Ferry with efficiency and minimal bloodshed.

In February 1860 Lee was ordered back to Texas to take temporary command of the Department of Texas. He proceeded to San Antonio, where he remained until replaced in December by the regular appointee, Brigadier General David E. Twiggs. Then Lee rode north to Fort Mason on the frontier, where he resumed command of the 2nd Cavalry. He performed his duties conscientiously during this last stay in Texas, but his attention was drawn elsewhere, for he watched with heavy heart as the clouds of secession and its consequences moved ominously into view.

Lee was in a deep quandary over the disturbing political conditions that had grown out of the slavery controversy. He was a soldier by profession, not a politician, philosopher, or theologian, and he left no statement of his full thoughts on the subject of slavery. What is known of his views on it comes from a few brief passages in private correspondence. They reveal that he had seriously reflected on the slavery problem and what could be done about it. He recognized it as the most momentous and difficult question of the age, one that had baffled the nation's leading statesmen from George Washington and Thomas Jefferson to Henry Clay and Abraham Lincoln. Lee's statements on the subject, like theirs, were sprinkled with ambiguities.

By now many southerners subscribed to the belief that slavery was a positive good in society. Lee did not share this view. He looked upon slavery itself as an evil. He had provided for the emancipation of the few slaves he owned. In his most meditative discussion of slavery, written in 1856 in a letter to his wife, he said, "In this enlightened age, there are few I believe, but what will acknowledge that slavery as an institution is a moral & political evil in any country." He added that he considered it a greater evil to whites than to blacks, who, he said, were immeasurably better off in American slavery than they would be if in Africa. He could see no human means of ending slavery, but said, "While we see the course of the final abolition of human slavery is onward, & we give it the aid of our prayers & all justifiable means within our power, we must leave the result in his hands who sees the end, who chooses to work by slow influences, & with whom two thousand years are but a single day."

Lee was quoted after the Civil War as denying that he had participated in it for the purpose of perpetuating slavery, that he was happy over the abolition of it, and that he would cheerfully have given up all he had lost if by so doing he could have brought an end to the institution. If he actually made this statement, he doubtless exaggerated what he would have been willing to do in order to eliminate slavery, but there is compelling evidence that he was sincere in saying he was happy about its elimination (though not over the manner in which this occurred), and that he had not fought in order to preserve it.

But all of Lee's views on slavery, whether of condemnation or justification, whether explicitly stated or implied, turned on what he later said was the overriding problem connected with abolishing the institution: what was to be done with the blacks if they should be set free. Late in the Civil War Lee would say that slavery was the best arrangement for them "as long as the two races are commingled."

To avoid a presentist judgment on Lee in this matter (that is, employing today's standards of judgment) requires placing his views in the context of his own times. No American political leader then had a workable solution to the problem of what to do with the blacks if they were freed; virtually all white Americans believed that their assimilation into the society at large was impossible.

Even Lincoln, the greatest statesman of the age, a persistent critic of slavery and an opponent of the spread of the institution, was at a complete loss over this question. He was not an abolitionist; he admitted he did not know what to do about slavery where it already existed. His expressed views on blacks would today be considered shockingly racist; he opposed granting citizenship to the black residents of his own state, Illinois; he never challenged the state's black exclusion legislation; and in speaking against the spread of slavery into the open portions of the nation he explained that these areas ought to be reserved for free, *white* settlers.

The mood of the nation would not wait upon the glacial moves of Providence that Lee hoped would bring a peaceful end to slavery. Fiery spirits were now demanding an immediate solution to the problem, and in a letter to his wife Lee spoke vehemently against the militant abolitionists, who, he believed, were seeking to foment a slave insurrection, a view shared by most southerners of the time.

Lee continued, "The consequences of their plans & purposes are clearly set forth, & they must also be aware that their object is both unlawful & entirely foreign to them and to their duty; for which they are irresponsible & unaccountable." They intended, he said, to accomplish their goal "through the agency of civil and servile war." This led him to broaden his focus to comment, "Is it not strange that the descendants of those pilgrim fathers who crossed the Atlantic to preserve their own freedom of opinion, have always proved themselves intolerant of the spiritual liberty of others?"

The most immediate and dangerous controversy in the slavery debate focused on whether slaveowners should have the right to carry their slave property into the Federal territories, areas not yet states and still under temporary government. Southerners claimed the right as being guaranteed by the Constitution, and a recent act of Congress creating the territories of Kansas and Nebraska had removed Federal restrictions against slavery in these territories. Lee endorsed the southern view, though he probably shared the belief of such eminent statesmen as Clay, John C. Calhoun, and Daniel Webster that the institution had reached its geographic limits, and that the controversy concerning the territories was actually a sectional political struggle.

Secession plunged Lee's mind and heart into turmoil, as it did the minds and hearts of immense numbers of Americans at the time, and especially those who lived in the upper South. Though he admitted what he considered to be the justice of southern resentment over the "denial of the equal rights of our citizens to the common territory of the commonwealth [that is, the Federal territories], he expressed his displeasure with the threats of secession being uttered by the states of the lower South.

When the secession of those states began actually to occur, he expressed his hope that his own state would stand fast: "I am particularly anxious that Virginia should keep right, as she was chiefly instrumental in the formation & inauguration of the

Constitution. So I could wish that she might be able to maintain it to save the Union." As for himself, he said he was unwilling to do what was wrong, at the bidding of either the South or the North.

Lee condemned secession as being revolution. Then, drawing upon the history of an earlier threat of secession, he said in particularly strong language, "When the New England States resisted Mr. Jeffersons Imbargo [*sic*] Law & the Hartford Convention assembled, secession was termed treason by a Virga [Virginia] statesman. What can it be now?"

He confided to a friend, "I wish to live under no other government [than that of the United States], and there is no sacrifice I am not ready to make for the preservation of the Union save that of honor. If a disruption takes place, I shall go back in sorrow to my people & share the misery of my native state." Then he added this line, the full significance of which may not have struck him at the moment: "Save in her [the native state's] defence there will be one less soldier in the world than now."

Again he wrote, "I can anticipate no greater calamity for this country than a dissolution of the Union. . . . I am willing to sacrifice everything but honor for its preservation. Secession is nothing but revolution. . . . Still a Union that can only be maintained by swords and bayonets, and in which strife and civil war are to take the place of brotherly love and kindness, has no charm for me. I shall mourn for my country, and for the welfare and progress of mankind. If the Union is dissolved and the government disrupted, I shall return to my native State and share the miseries of my people, and, save in defence, will draw my sword no more."

Lee was at Fort Mason when he received War Department orders to report by April 1 to General in Chief Winfield Scott in Washington. As Lee was leaving, a fellow officer asked whether he intended to join the South or the North. In a hasty reply, Lee made his most starkly ambiguous and ominous statement regarding his intentions for the future: "I shall never bear arms against the Union, but it may be necessary for me to carry a musket in defence of my native state, Virginia."

Whether he sensed the purpose of his recall to the capital is not known, but it was soon made clear in a series of conversations with General Scott and other dignitaries in Washington. Lee was being groomed for high military command in the event of an outbreak of hostilities with the seceded southern states.

On April 12–14 the feared outbreak occurred as Confederate batteries bombarded Fort Sumter in Charleston harbor into surrender. Four days later Lee received from President Lincoln's representative, Francis Preston Blair, Sr., the offer of command of a United States army being assembled to suppress secession and hold the southern states in the Union by force. Courteously and sorrowfully Lee declined the offer and explained that, though he opposed secession, he could take no part in an invasion of the South. He then called upon General Scott and told him what he had done. Sadly the old general who so admired Lee the soldier said, "Lee, you have made the mistake of your life." He also told Lee the time had come for him to resign from the United States Army.

Lee was now obliged to choose definitely between conflicting loyalties, to make what the eulogistic biographer Thomas Nelson Page called "the choice of Hercules." There is no reason to doubt that this decision cut Lee to the heart as similar decisions did a host of his friends both in and out of the army. For weeks he had struggled with what to do if his own beloved Virginia should secede. He had reached the irreconcilable conclusions that he could not fight against the Union, yet that he must fight, if necessary, to defend the soil of Virginia. The state had seceded on April 17, and Lee, knowing President Lincoln's purpose, realized that an invasion by Union forces was imminent.

After midnight the day following the offer of the Union command, Lee sat down in his room at Arlington and wrote a letter of one sentence to the Secretary of War resigning his commission in the United States Army. Then Lee wrote to General Scott informing him of this action and thanking him for all past kindnesses. At the end of this letter Lee repeated the statement indicating unmistakably the direction in which his heart was bearing him. He said, "Save in defence of my native state, I never again desire to draw my sword."

"Save in defence of my native state." These words summed up Lee's supreme loyalty and forecast his conduct in the coming struggle. As much as he loved the Union—and he did love it, having served it with intense dedication throughout his career, having risked his life selflessly in its behalf in the Mexican War, and having "wept tears of blood" over the issue of secession—he now joined his fate with the fate of Virginia. Though he did not say it explicitly, he obviously had come to accept state revolution as a legitimate measure of self-defense. He must, he said, side either for or against his own people. And, "I cannot raise my hand against my birthplace, my home, my children." He could well have added the words uttered by his father at the time of the American Revolution: "Virginia is my country. Her will I obey, however lamentable the fate to which it may subject me."

On the same day that Robert E. Lee resigned from the United States service he received a summons to a conference with Governor John Letcher of Virginia. Two days later Lee left Arlington forever, bound for Richmond and an unknown destiny.

Some of Lee's critics imply that at the time he made his fateful decision to resign he had already been in negotiation with the Virginia authorities. There is no documentary evidence of this, and even if he had been in correspondence with them, the suggestion that he was induced by self-interest to turn down the offer of the top Union command in order to accept a position in the Virginia forces makes little sense. He was keenly aware that he was placing his own welfare in jeopardy. To his army associates, including those who remained loyal to the Union, his character made unthinkable any kind of bargaining by him on this occasion.

Yet a man of his training and record had to have sensed that the state would call upon his leadership in her hour of crisis. A month earlier the Confederate authorities had offered him an assignment as a brigadier general. If he received the letter containing the offer, he ignored it. But he could not have been surprised when Governor Letcher offered him an appointment as commander of the military and naval forces of Virginia, with the rank of major general. Having already made his decision to fight with his people if they should be assailed, Lee accepted the offer without hesitation.

He was now fifty-four years old, but he still seemed to be in the full vigor of life. He retained the trim figure and springy step of his youth, for he had kept active in dancing, riding, swimming, and athletic contests, even competing with his sons in high jumping when he was in his forties. Though not a man of great brute strength, his powers of mental and physical endurance were remarkable: he possibly surpassed every other American soldier of his time in his ability to stay on his feet or in the saddle day after day under the weight of physical, intellectual, and emotional stress.

He had, however, received a warning symptom, the significance of which was not then apparent. A few months earlier he had suffered from a nagging pain in his right arm, which he diagnosed as rheumatism and dismissed by saying it was uncomfortable, "but more to be apprehended as the harbinger of future evil." These words may have been far more prophetic then he knew.

His countenance was now reserved and his hair flecked with gray, though his mustache was still black. The passage of the years had enhanced his already striking appearance. A short time before, while he was the superintendent at West Point, a cadet described him as the handsomest man he had ever known, "just like a marble model," a simile that later would be used by both his admirers and his critics, though the cadet's mother, who was personally acquainted with Lee, insightfully replied at the time, "Handsome, yes, but not like marble. Colonel Lee is very human, kind, calm, and definite." Her word *calm* was applicable most of the time. On rare occasions, however, he displayed a fierce anger that showed in his flushed face and the swelling veins of his neck. Ordinarily his anger remained in check to his exceptional personal discipline and composure.

An observer in 1861 said Lee was "the noblest-looking man I had ever gazed upon. . . . handsome beyond all men I have ever seen." Unquestionably, Lee's electric force of leadership derived in part from his Olympian looks and bearing.

Intellectually also, Lee was at the height of his power. Always quick in learning, balanced in judgment, prompt and sure in decision, and thorough in performance, he now had at his call a fund of knowledge and experience acquired throughout a professional career of more than thirty years. He was a man of action rather than of books, yet he had continuously expanded his mind with reading from the literary masters. Fully as important as his mental acuteness was his emotional stability, which enabled him to exercise immense presence of mind when under stress.

Lee possessed one other internal source of strength for the trial by fire that lay ahead of him. He was devoutly religious. Reared an Episcopalian and under the influence of his mother's piety, he nevertheless had delayed being confirmed into the church until two of his daughters were old enough for confirmation. In the summer of 1853 he and they presented themselves together. Thereafter he attended services as regularly as circumstances permitted, and he read the Scriptures and prayed daily.

Underneath Lee's outward manifestations of religious grace lay an abiding faith in the will and wisdom of the Almighty to direct the affairs of men to their ultimate good. He filled his letters written to his wife from camp and campaign with invocations of God's blessings and affirmations of subjection to the divine will. A typical line to his wife said, "May He continue His mercies to us both and all our children, relatives and friends, and in His own good time unite us in His worship, if not on earth, forever in heaven." Writing to console a soldier upon the death of the soldier's young son, Lee said that, though grief-stricken, he considered it "far better for the child to be called by its heavenly Creator into His presence in its purity and innocence, unpolluted by sins, and uncontaminated by the vices of the world."

Religion produced in Lee a sense of fatalism toward the issues of life. He believed that after man had done all within his power to bring about a desired result, it would be decided by God. Lee was convinced that God alone could purge the world of evil, and that he would, at his appointed hour, rid it even of the curse of human bondage. Lee prayed that the nation might be spared the ordeal of war, but, in a statement that anticipated one of Lincoln's most famous utterances, Lee said that if war should come, it would be "a necessary expiation, perhaps, of our national sins." Finally, he believed that the outcome of the sectional struggle itself lay in God's hands.

Lee looked to the Lord for support and guidance in bearing the heavy personal responsibility that now rested upon him. He said, "May God enable me to perform my duty and not suffer me to be tempted beyond my strength." His religious faith made him a leader serene in the midst of adversity and self-assured in the face of seemingly insurmountable odds.

On the morning of April 23, 1861, Lee assumed the defense of Virginia.

"Lee the Invincible"

Commonwealth Commander and Confederate General

Lee now found himself responsible for defending an area more than four hundred miles in width containing a population of more than 1.5 million, one third of which was black slaves. Auspiciously for Lee and Virginia, the state possessed a fairly well-developed militia on which a defense could be established. But this had to be done with the utmost haste, for President Lincoln had given the seceded states only twenty days in which to return to their allegiance, and he was mustering armies to enforce his decision. Lee was not deceived by friendly but idle boasts into scorning the seriousness or magnitude of his undertaking. He warned his associates that the people of the North would fight steadfastly to preserve the Union and that the states of the South could not rely on the hope of European intervention. He wrote his wife that the struggle might last ten years.

Many southern newspaper editors and a number of southern political figures, including the ex-governor of Virginia, Henry A. Wise, favored an immediate invasion of the North in the hope of winning the war before northern resources could be fully mobilized. Disregarding these Hotspurs, Lee made the important decision to remain on the defensive and gain as much time as possible to prepare for the war. Then he set about systematically to occupy and defend the most strategic points and routes of invasion into Virginia, to organize an efficient staff and corps of officers, and to mobilize, arm, and train the state's manpower into an effective combat force.

He turned first to Virginia's exposed coastline and rushed the available naval and engineering officers and militia troops to strengthen and hold Norfolk and its valuable navy yard, which had been taken earlier by state forces, and to erect fortifications and batteries on the Rappahannock, York, and James Rivers, the natural avenues of penetration into the heart of the state. Next he sent Colonel Thomas J. Jackson, the future "Stonewall," to take command of militia troops at Harpers Ferry in order to guard this doorway to the Shenandoah Valley and to salvage the vital armaments machinery from the seized United States arsenal there.

Lee began also to concentrate troops at Manassas Junction, which was located on the Orange and Alexandria Railroad some thirty miles from Washington, and which lay in the direct line of march to Richmond. Finally, he dispatched officers to western Virginia in an effort to rally the population there to the Confederate cause.

While Lee hastened the state's troops to their assigned stations, he also created the departments of the general staff (adjutant general, quartermaster, subsistence, medical, and pay), and from Governor Letcher he obtained commissions for various Virginia officers who had resigned from the United States Army and who would later make their mark in the Confederate service. These included Joseph E. Johnston, John Bankhead Magruder, and Richard S. Ewell.

With an officer corps established, Lee then called for the general mobilization of the state's manpower, and within a month he enlisted some forty thousand volunteers, issued them muskets from Virginia arsenals and from those purchased or seized, and began a program of training in hastily constructed camps and schools. He armed his light artillery with cannon from the state armories and his heavy artillery with ordnance captured in the Norfolk navy yard. He was able to collect enough ammunition from state supplies, from stocks captured at Norfolk, and from various unidentified sources to ready his forces for one engagement.

By early June, Lee's mobilization of Virginia forces was completed, and the work of perfecting their arming and training was progressing at a feverish pace. He was fortunate in that the Federal government was not able to mount a determined offensive against him. Only in the western region of the state—an area of overwhelming Unionist sympathy that had provided him few volunteers—were his meager forces obliged to retire in the face of Federal advances.

Scarcely had Lee finished the mustering of Virginia troops when the time came for him to turn them over to the Confederate authorities, for Virginia was now a member of the Confederacy, Richmond was the capital of the new would-be nation, and Confederate regiments were already arriving in Virginia from other places. Lee's rank of brigadier general in the Confederacy, activated after he resigned from the United States Army, ran concurrent with his rank in the Virginia state forces, and the Confederate regiments in Virginia were placed under his command as they appeared.

In May he was elevated by the Confederate Congress to the rank of full general, though this commission was not confirmed until August 31, when it was dated in such a way as to place him third in the order of seniority among the original full generals of the Confederacy, behind the elderly Adjutant General Samuel Cooper and Lee's former regimental commander, Albert Sidney Johnston, and ahead of Joseph E. Johnston and P. G. T. Beauregard. On June 8 Governor Letcher formally transferred the armed forces of Virginia to the Confederacy.

Lee could look with justifiable pride on his accomplishments as commander of the Virginia forces. In seven weeks he had provided the state with effective coastal and river fortifications and the makings of a formidable army. Except for the western counties, which may have been indefensible anyway, he had posted his troops wisely for the state's protection. Considering the scope of the task and the brevity of the time available, he had wrought a near miracle of mobilization. A Richmond editor aptly lauded him as "the sagacious, intrepid and high-souled chieftain of Virginia."

Now that his services to Virginia as such were ended, he was available for full-time Confederate duty. Temporarily, after the transfer of the Virginia forces to the Confederacy, he served Confederate President Jefferson Davis in the position of military advisor and handyman.

Lee was in this capacity when on July 21, 1861, the first full-scale engagement of the Civil War occurred: the first battle of Manassas, or Bull Run. Although he did not participate directly in this Confederate victory, it was, to a considerable degree, the product of his work, for he was the person who selected Manassas Junction as the point for the concentration of Confederate troops; who mobilized, trained, and armed one fourth of the Confederates who fought there; and who recommended the junction of the command of Joseph E. Johnston from the Shenandoah Valley with that of Beauregard that made the victory possible.

A week after the battle at Manassas Lee received his first assignment to Confederate field duty when he was sent by President Davis to oversee operations in western Virginia. Lee undoubtedly shouldered this burden with misgivings, for western Virginia was the one area where he had been unable to accomplish anything positive as the commander of Virginia state forces. Moreover, the present assignment contained the seeds of failure in that, though he was given the responsibility for operations in the area, he was not actually placed in command of the troops there. Two weeks earlier the Confederate forces in the area, under Brigadier General Robert S. Garnett, were surprised and routed at Rich Mountain and beaten at Laurel Hill by Lee's old comrade in arms, Major General George B. McClellan.

The Federals now held Cheat Mountain, a strong point overlooking the Parkersburg-Staunton turnpike. From this position they also threatened the vital Virginia Central and Virginia and Tennessee Railroads, and they stood poised to invade the Shenandoah Valley, the chief granary of Virginia.

Lee purposed to combine or coordinate the command of Brigadier General W. W. Loring, successor to Garnett, who was killed in the withdrawal from Laurel Hill, with the small forces of Brigadier Generals John B. Floyd and Henry A. Wise, both of them former governors of Virginia who had been authorized by President Davis to raise volunteer units in the region and who were operating as virtually independent commanders. Loring's troops held the mountain passes around Huntersville, where he had established his headquarters, and opposed the victorious Federals on Cheat Mountain.

Floyd and Wise were both near Carnifix Ferry in the Kanawha Valley facing a Federal column that was pressing up the valley so as to threaten the Virginia and Tennessee Railroad at Lynchburg. This railroad was the Confederacy's one direct line between Virginia and the states west of the Appalachians. Lee hoped to mount a series of counteroffensives that would dislodge the Federals from their commanding positions and possibly drive them beyond the Ohio River.

He found the scattered Confederates ill-equipped and demoralized, the commanders themselves contentious and envious of one another. Loring resented Lee's presence at Huntersville, and only tardily and grudgingly executed a movement planned by Lee against the Federals on Cheat Mountain. When on September 11–13 the Confederates finally advanced, Lee's complicated enveloping attack, involving the concerted movements of five separate columns, miscarried completely. The Federals remained undisturbed in their stronghold.

Despairing of success at Cheat Mountain, Lee now shifted his attention to the situation in the Kanawha Valley fifty miles to the southwest, where the Federals were being reinforced for a renewal of their drive. Their commander was now Brigadier General William S. Rosecrans, who succeeded McClellan when that officer was called to Washington to become the general in chief of Union armies. Instructing Loring to move to the Kanawha Valley with the main body of his force, leaving only enough troops to secure the positions around Huntersville, Lee rode at once to the camps of Floyd and Wise in the valley.

He reached Floyd's headquarters on September 21, only to discover that Wise and Floyd stubbornly refused either to combine their little commands or to cooperate in action. For four days Lee vainly urged them to join forces, but it was not until September 25, after Wise had received orders from the Confederate War Department to turn over his troops to Floyd and report to Richmond for reassignment, that Lee was able to achieve the junction that he desired. Four days later Loring arrived with the bulk of his command, giving Lee sufficient strength to attack Rosecrans with confidence. Instead, plagued by the shortage of supplies and the deplorable condition of the roads, he chose to take a defensive position on Big Sewell Mountain and invite a Federal assault.

Rosecrans warily refused to walk into the trap. Withdrawing down the valley, he began to reconcentrate troops against the weakened Confederate positions in the Huntersville area. Lee made one brief effort to pursue, then gave it up because of the near impassability of the roads and the want of transportation and equipment. Fearing a renewed threat to the Confederates around Huntersville, he ordered Loring on October 20 back to his original sector and placed the remaining troops in the

Kanawha Valley on a strict defensive. By now Lee's campaign to expel the Federals from the western part of Virginia was stalled.

In a referendum held on October 24 a majority of the voters of the region elected to withdraw from the state of Virginia and remain within the Union. With all hope gone of retrieving the area for the Confederacy, Davis ordered Lee back to Richmond.

Whether by any course Lee could have expelled the Federals from western Virginia is debatable. The shortage of Confederate troops and equipment, the miserable condition of the roads, the enemy's advantage of position, and the mood of the population were all against him. Yet he failed personally in two ways. In his unwillingness to issue peremptory orders to his subordinates or to remove them when they hesitated in obeying his instructions, he lost promising opportunities for striking the Federals an effective blow. In prematurely assuming the defensive in the Kanawha Valley, he lost a chance of defeating Rosecrans there. Lee made an important accomplishment in stopping the Federal threat to the railroads and the Shenandoah Valley. But because he achieved no spectacular feat of arms, he returned to Richmond with his prestige eroded. To many, he had become "Granny" Lee.

Fortunately for Lee and the Confederacy, President Davis did not share the critics' views of him. Instead, on October 31 Davis welcomed him cordially back to Richmond, and five days later he dispatched him on another important mission, assigning him to take command of a newly created department comprising the Atlantic coast of South Carolina, Georgia, and eastern Florida.

Lee arrived in Charleston on November 7 to learn that the forts guarding the entrance to Port Royal Sound, lying between Charleston and Savannah, were under attack by a Federal fleet and could not be held. Ordering the beleaguered garrisons withdrawn to interior positions, he turned to the task of preparing a defense for the entire three-hundred-mile southern Atlantic coastline. Possibly because he found this service more agreeable to his experience as an engineer, he now showed none of the hesitancy that had marked his western Virginia campaign.

He promptly decided that three major courses ought to be followed. The forts guarding Savannah and Charleston ought to be strengthened; the navigable rivers ought to be obstructed against the use of Federal vessels; and the 12,300 scattered Confederate troops assigned to the defense of the area ought to be concentrated at the most vulnerable points along the railroad that connected Charleston and Savannah. After a quick but thorough reconnaissance of the area, Lee decided that his program could best be carried out by withdrawing the guns and troops from most of the outlying positions where they were originally located and were exposed to enemy naval fire, by reinforcing the forts guarding the approaches to the two cities, and by constructing an interior line of heavy earthworks to protect the exposed lower stretch of the railroad in the vicinity of Savannah.

For four hectic months Lee supervised the construction of these defenses. He was fortunate in that his Federal opponents, Flag Officer Samuel F. Du Pont, commander of the blockading naval squadron, and General Thomas W. Sherman, commander of the army forces, made no determined attacks against him. A more aggressive foe might have overwhelmed the unfinished positions in the early stages of Lee's command, but by the time he left the department he was unquestionably capable of carrying out a promise that he made in a letter of March 2, 1862, to his daughter Annie: "But if our men will stand to their work, we shall give [the enemy] trouble and damage them yet." His planning proved to be eminently sound. Not until the war was almost over would these cities and positions fall, and then only to an army approaching from the interior.

He had no opportunity to try his works and strategy. On the same day that he penned his letter to Annie he received in Savannah a telegram from Davis instructing him to return to

Richmond, which he obeyed at once. His experience in the Atlantic Coastal Department had been one of drudgery rather than excitement, yet it had provided him an exercise in independent command, where, though he still displayed a reluctance to impose his will upon stubborn subordinates, he proved his initiative and energy in conceiving and executing large plans. This experience had one other important effect on Lee's thinking: in spite of the complaints of those who held earthworks in contempt and came to jeer him as the "King of Spades," he left this service with a renewed faith in the effectiveness of field fortifications to enable troops to oppose superior numbers and armament.

He returned at a critical hour in the fortunes of the Confederacy. Within the previous month the garrison on Roanoke Island guarding the entrance to the North Carolina sounds had fallen, exposing an important reach of the Atlantic coast below Richmond. Beyond the Appalachians, General Albert Sidney Johnston had lost Forts Henry and Donelson on the Tennessee and Cumberland Rivers, leaving the western Confederate theater open to penetration. Johnston was desperately trying to collect his scattered forces in northern Mississippi for a counterblow against the invaders.

Closer to home, the greatest army ever assembled on the continent, more than one hundred thousand men, was being drilled by General McClellan for a renewed drive on Richmond. In the midst of these ominous developments, Lee on March 13 was appointed to take charge, "under the direction of the President," of the military operations of the armies of the Confederacy.

This assignment did not place Lee in actual command of any army at all. Indeed, the move was made by Davis to avoid the necessity of creating the position of general in chief, which the Confederate Congress was now urging. Lee found himself once again in the capacity of military advisor to the president. Fearing that he would wear an empty title, Lee wrote that he could see neither advantage nor pleasure in the job. His forebodings were, to a degree, borne out, for he quickly found himself saddled with countless minor and vexing details but without any command authority, never free to initiate and carry out a complete plan of his own.

Yet, even in so frustrating a position, he offered counsel that showed deep insight into the nature of war, and he supported certain measures that would immensely strengthen the South for the ordeal that it faced. Seeing immediately the importance of the western theater, he recommended sending additional troops there and said, "If the Mississippi Valley is lost, the Atlantic states would be ruined." His advice to General Johnston in Mississippi was sound and timely: he wrote with infinite tact to say he hoped Johnston would be able to concentrate his forces and strike Major General U. S. Grant's army before it could be reinforced. Johnston did as Lee suggested, and as he himself had already determined to do, with the result that the battle of Shiloh, or Pittsburg Landing (April 6–7, 1862), though ultimately a Union victory for reasons beyond Lee's control, came remarkably close to destroying the main Union army in the West.

One of the most important steps taken by Lee during this period of his career was his support of conscription for the mobilization of the military manpower of the South. This action demonstrated unusual foresight. The United States government had never resorted to national conscription; many Americans believed it unconstitutional. Many of the civil leaders of the Confederacy opposed it as being a violation of states' rights, the fundamental political principle of the new nation.

Lee showed here also that he was capable of looking beyond the textbook in his own concepts of warfare, for the most influential military theorists of the era held that wars ought to be fought by professional armies. Lee, on the other hand, affirmed in 1862 a principle of total mobilization that harked back to the French

Revolution but would not again be put into full effect until the world wars of the twentieth century. He said, "Since the whole duty of the [Confederate] nation [will] be war until independence [is] secured, the whole nation should for a time be converted into an army, the producers to feed and the soldiers to fight." His endorsement of conscription after the losses at Shiloh and elsewhere helped to persuade the Confederate Congress to adopt the measure in April 1862.

Lee's most urgent problem as Davis's advisor was the threat of an immediate and overpowering attack on Richmond by McClellan's army. Even before Lee left Savannah to return to the capital, General Joseph E. Johnston, commanding the Confederate army in northern Virginia, had abandoned the position at Manassas and withdrawn behind the Rappahannock River only sixty miles from Richmond. Now a strong Federal force was reported arriving by transports at Old Point, Virginia, apparently in preparation for a drive to turn Johnston's position by advancing upon the capital along the peninsula formed by the York and James Rivers.

With the enemy forces temporarily divided between northern Virginia and the peninsula, Lee wished to take advantage of the Confederacy's interior position by rushing the bulk of Johnston's troops to strike the Federals on the lower peninsula, then back to the Rappahannock in time to meet an attack by the Federals there. This was admittedly risky, since well-timed offensives by both enemy forces might catch the Confederate main body on the move and inflict a catastrophic defeat before it could be committed to decisive action.

Lee's proposal gave a glimpse of his strategic thinking and of his remarkable audacity in pursuit of it. It was too bold for Johnston, who preferred instead to abandon the lower peninsula altogether and to concentrate as great a Confederate army as possible for the defense of Richmond, even drawing all of the troops out of the Carolinas and Georgia for this purpose.

Lee opposed Johnston's strategy, for he reasoned that the enemy's superiority in numbers and transport facilities would enable them to mass an irresistible force against the Confederates at Richmond, and that a prolonged siege there would seal the fate of the city. Persuaded by Lee, Davis vetoed Johnston's plan and ordered him to shift the main part of his army to the peninsula and to engage the enemy before they reached Richmond. At the same time, Davis turned over to Lee the conduct of the operations of the one body of troops left on the Rappahannock (Ewell's division) and of Stonewall Jackson's small force, which since Manassas had been posted to guard the Shenandoah Valley.

Lee was not actually in command of these units, whose primary missions were to secure their immediate fronts. He nevertheless now determined to employ them in such a fashion that they might also support Johnston's efforts against McClellan's advance up the peninsula. The surest way to do this was to prevent McClellan from being reinforced by a Federal corps that remained north of the Rappahannock under the command of General Irvin McDowell.

In order to divert McDowell, Lee adopted a tried-and-true stratagem, that of threatening the enemy's homeland with invasion. On April 21 he wrote to Jackson suggesting that this stern commander, reinforced by Ewell's division, attack the Federals in the Valley, and, if possible, move forward as if he intended to cross the Potomac into Maryland or Pennsylvania. "I have hoped," said Lee, "in the present divided condition of the enemy's forces that a successful blow may be dealt them by a rapid combination of our troops before they can be strengthened themselves either in position or by reenforcements."

Lee was obliged to wait for more than a month to learn the outcome of his plan. Meanwhile, McClellan's deliberate but formidable advance up the peninsula occupied all the energies of the Confederate leaders. By the final week in May the forces of Johnston and McClellan were ready to join in battle for the possession of

Richmond, while Lee was aware that McDowell was marching south to throw his weight into the scales. If he should succeed in reinforcing McClellan, the Confederate army of approximately seventy-two thousand would be opposed by more than twice its numbers.

On May 26 Lee received a welcome message from Jackson saying that he had routed the Federals in the Valley and was moving toward the Potomac. Three additional days of suspense elapsed before Lee received the word that he yearned to hear: that McDowell's column had halted in its tracks and was now returning to its position north of the Rappahannock. The quiet man in Richmond whose planning was largely responsible for this turn of events must have breathed a prayer of relief and gratitude.

On the afternoon of May 31, while both Lee and President Davis were at Johnston's headquarters, the long-expected battle for Richmond began south of the Chickahominy River only six miles from the city. With Johnston absent somewhere at the front and the din of combat increasing by the hour, Lee and the president anxiously awaited the result of the fighting. When at dusk no word had arrived from the commander, they rode forward in search of him. They found him in the midst of confusion and a throng of wounded men moving to the rear, borne on a litter, too severely wounded to discuss his plans or the course of the battle. Seeing that the second in command, General Gustavus Smith, was un-informed and indecisive, Davis now made his supreme decision of the entire war. He assigned Lee to the command of the embattled Confederate army.

This was a momentous step for the future of the Confederacy. Whether it was a wise one is debatable. It placed Lee in the kind of position he, like most other military men, most desired, that of combat command. In this capacity he would achieve prodigies in the field, but the assignment removed him from the command and control center of the southern forces. It deprived the Confederacy of his strategic guidance at the seat of government. Some scholars believe he would have rendered more valuable service there, where he would have been in position to play a role similar to that of the chief of staff of today. Notwithstanding Lee's later accomplishments, his foremost biographer, Douglas Southall Freeman, concludes that there were few if any periods of his career in which he contributed more to Confederate success than while he was in Richmond.

"Lee the Invincible"

Lee inherited an army in the chaos of an unfinished and desperate battle. Addressing his forces as "The Army of Northern Virginia," a name that was to become legendary, he ordered them to cease action and return to their previously fortified positions while he planned a counteroffensive according to his own strategy. At first he considered holding Richmond temporarily with part of his troops and rushing heavy reinforcements to Jackson for a determined invasion of the North by way of the Shenandoah Valley. When he was obliged to abandon this idea for want of sufficient strength, he reverted to his earlier plan of feigning an invasion of the North in order to immobilize McDowell while concentrating all available forces in an attack on McClellan. On June 11 he dispatched a few additional regiments to Jackson along with orders to strike the Federals in the Valley one more blow, then bring the bulk of his army to the peninsula to join in the grand offensive.

Lee succeeded spectacularly in keeping the Federal forces divided and in concentrating the Confederates in an attack against McClellan. Armed with information provided by Brigadier

General J. E. B. "Jeb" Stuart's daring ride with his cavalry around McClellan's entire army, and reinforced by Jackson with eighteen thousand troops from the Valley, Lee struck the Union force in quick succession in the battles of Mechanicsville, Gaines's Mill, Savage Station, Frayser's Farm, and Malvern Hill (June 26–July 2). He failed to accomplish what he had hoped: the destruction of the Federal army by turning its right flank at Mechanicsville, or by catching it on the move in the following engagements as it withdrew to a more secure base—Harrison's Landing—on the James River. Derelictions by his subordinate commanders, faulty work by his inexperienced staff, and Lee's overly complicated tactical plan involving converging columns along unfamiliar roads perhaps deprived him of a decisive triumph on the peninsula.

None of the separate engagements was a clear Confederate tactical victory; Malvern Hill was a distinct Confederate repulse. Confederate casualties were extremely heavy, an aggregate of twenty thousand in contrast to the stronger opponent's sixteen thousand. Lee had shown, particularly at Malvern Hill, a questionable willingness to launch frontal attacks. Yet without his audacity and will there would have been no counteroffensive, and the counteroffensive was a strategic victory of incalculable proportions. It saved the Confederate capital and forced the Union authorities to abandon the peninsular campaign altogether. Coming in the wake of such Confederate losses as Shiloh, Memphis, and New Orleans, with southern morale plummeting disastrously, Lee's electrifying success in Virginia may have saved the Confederacy itself.

Lee was undoubtedly aware of the wider significance of his feat, that he had forged the Army of Northern Virginia into a weapon strong and keen and that he himself had emerged as a bold, resourceful, and inspiring commander. In the eyes of the public and of his troops the King of Spades had been transformed into a formidable attacker.

Lee now had to consider his options. He knew that the checking of McClellan's drive for Richmond gave the Confederacy a respite only, not a permanent reprieve. Lee was keenly aware that any form of strictly defensive strategy would surrender the initiative to the enemy, allow him to mass an overwhelming force, and to strike at the time, place, and manner of his own choosing. To prevent this, Lee must maneuver his forces so as to hold his opponent at a distance from Richmond and at the same time take advantage of all opportunities to deliver crippling blows against isolated enemy contingents.

During the lull in fighting that followed the battles on the peninsula, Lee reorganized his army into two wings commanded by Major Generals James Longstreet and Jackson, with the cavalry under the dashing Stuart. Meanwhile, Lee remained ever alert for any shift in the Federal forces that would permit him to attack with a promise of success. On July 12 he received news that prompted him to alter the dispositions of his troops and begin the course of events that would lead to his next counteroffensive.

He now learned that a powerful Union column under Major General John Pope had moved south from Washington and seized Culpeper Court House on the Orange and Alexandria Railroad only seventy miles above Richmond. Sensing that the next northern drive would be made by Pope, Lee decided to rush the bulk of his army north to strike the Federals there before they could be significantly reinforced by troops that were being transferred to them from McClellan's army on the peninsula.

Lee hoped to trap Pope's army between the Rapidan River at its front and the Rappahannock at its rear. Leaving twenty thousand men to guard the capital from a Federal move on the peninsula, Lee concentrated fifty-five thousand troops by rail at Gordonsville, and from there he moved on August 25 against Pope in the second battle of Manassas.

Lee sent Jackson on a prodigious march through Thoroughfare Gap in the Bull Run Mountains to turn Pope's right flank and seize and destroy the Federal supply depot at Manassas Junction behind the Federal line. When Pope laboriously pivoted his army and attacked Jackson, who had secured his troops in an unfinished railroad cut, Lee followed Jackson with the remainder of his army, joined his forces on the field, and directed Longstreet's wing against Pope's exposed flank in a shattering blow (August 29–30) that sent the defeated Federal columns reeling northward into the Washington defenses.

Lee's decision to abandon the peninsula with most of his army and concentrate on Pope revealed an uncanny capacity for anticipating what the enemy planned to do, and an extraordinary boldness in acting on this anticipation. Lee's decision to divide his army in the presence of a more powerful foe and send Jackson around Pope's flank violated the orthodox rules of warfare by exposing the separate wings to the danger of being destroyed piecemeal by the concentrated Union force between them. Lee explained this action by saying, "The disparity . . . between the contending forces renders the risks unavoidable."

Second Manassas was a brilliant strategic, operational, and tactical victory for Lee. It was a strategic victory in that it aborted another major Union drive to seize the Confederate capital; an operational victory in Lee's ability to outmaneuver his opponent in the movement and deployment of his forces; a tactical victory in the skill with which the actual combat occurred, particularly Lee's success in uniting the wings of his army in the midst of the engagement, something that Napoleon had said was one of the most difficult accomplishments in warfare. Moreover, by inflicting substantially more casualties than he suffered (some 13,825 Union to 8,350 Confederate) Lee demonstrated that a bold and skillful employment of terrain, mobility, surprise, and mass could overcome the theoretically inherent advantage of the tactical defensive.

With the threat to Richmond momentarily removed, Lee made a decision to carry the war to the enemy by invading Union soil.

He believed such a campaign would benefit the cause of the South in a number of ways. His immediate goals were to confound the Union leaders and prevent or delay a renewal of their massive drive on Richmond, and to find provisions for his hungry army in the rich agricultural countryside of Maryland and Pennsylvania.

His larger aims were to bring Maryland, a state of divided sympathies, over to the Confederate side, and possibly to influence the governments of England and France to intervene on behalf of the Confederacy. He had something else in mind also. He was keenly aware that the South lacked the strength to conquer the North, that Confederate success must be achieved by measures short of absolute military victory, measures that would take advantage of northern war weariness and sagging confidence. With this in mind he recommended that Davis issue a peace offer to accompany the campaign.

Lee's proposed operation depended on decisiveness and speed to take advantage of the enemy's disorganization and demoralization following the defeat at Second Manassas. The campaign needed to be carried out as an exploitation or continuation of the recent victory. Aware that every hour was precious, Lee began immediately to move his army toward his objective. Recognizing the political and diplomatic aspects of a movement beyond the Confederate border, he notified Davis so that the march could be halted if the president disapproved. Davis did not disapprove. Six days after Second Manassas Lee began crossing his troops into Maryland.

Proceeding according to the Napoleonic precept that an army ought to be dispersed for marching and concentrated for fighting, Lee split his force by sending Jackson west to seize Harpers Ferry and the Baltimore and Ohio Railroad at that place, thereby also ensuring himself a line of communication by way of the Shenandoah Valley. He ordered detachments from Longstreet's wing to seize and hold the commanding heights near the mouth of the

Shenandoah. The entire army was then to reunite beyond the Potomac and march to Harrisburg, Pennsylvania, where the Pennsylvania Railroad, the one remaining direct link between the northeast and midwest, would be severed.

In adopting this course, Lee wagered his own boldness against the timidity of his opponent, McClellan, whom Lincoln had restored to the top Union command. Lee said, "The Federal army will not be prepared for offensive operations—or [McClellan] will not think it so—for three or four weeks. Before that time I hope to be on the Susquehanna."

But Lee's expectations all went awry. The people of Maryland turned a deaf ear to his overture of liberation, and, more alarming at that moment, McClellan moved against him with an unaccustomed speed and certainty. Prodded by Lincoln, and informed of Lee's plans by the chance capture of a copy of his orders found wrapped around some cigars, the Union commander sensed a splendid opportunity to destroy the separate segments of the Confederate army in turn before they could be reunited. When he read the order he exclaimed, "Here is a piece of paper with which if I cannot whip 'Bobby Lee,' I will be willing to go home." By September 14 McClellan's columns, an aggregate of ninety thousand, were marching confidently toward Sharpsburg, Maryland, where Lee with only twenty thousand troops awaited the arrival of the rest of his army.

Desperate as Lee's situation appeared to be, with his army divided and the Potomac between its wings, he kept his composure admirably. By dispatching a portion of his available infantry to reinforce Stuart's cavalry in contesting the Federals movement through the South Mountain gaps, he delayed their advance and purchased time for Jackson's main body to join him after a severe night march from Harpers Ferry. Deployed across an angle in the Potomac, which lay to the rear, the Confederate army of some forty thousand on the seventeenth beat off the Federals' repeated assaults in the battle of Antietam, or Sharpsburg, the bloodiest day of the Civil War. Lee's faith in his opponent's timidity was partially justified; McClellan held almost one fourth of his entire strength out of the battle to guard his left flank against a feared counterattack. Even so, he was finally repulsed by precisely such an operation staged at dusk by a lone Confederate division (Major General A. P. Hill's) that had just arrived from Harpers Ferry.

Lee remained boldly, or as some would say, rashly, in position for another day, then retired unmolested beyond the Potomac when McClellan chose not to renew the encounter. Antietam was a tactical victory for Lee, whose conduct on the field was a model of precision and presence of mind. But it was a victory dearly bought (ten thousand Confederate casualties to thirteen thousand Union casualties), and it was a strategic victory for the Union because it wrecked Lee's invasion of the North, aborted the anticipated welcome of Maryland, killed the hope of European recognition, and forced the war back upon southern soil. It had another effect that Lee had no way of being aware of: it was enough of a Union victory for Lincoln to feel justified in issuing his preliminary Emancipation Proclamation.

Lee did, however, gain a certain immediate advantage from the battle. Like Second Manassas, it nullified a potential Union advance. The carnage so shocked McClellan that he made no immediate move against the Confederates, though he had ample strength to do so. When he was still tactically idle a month later, complaining that his horses were too tired for a move, Lincoln replied cuttingly, "Will you pardon me for asking what the horses of your army have done since the battle of Antietam that would fatigue anything?" Eventually, McClellan's tardiness in mounting a fresh offensive would cost him the command.

Lee's image among his troops and among the southern population remained largely untarnished; their admiration for his courage and bearing in the heat of battle rose to new heights. Taking advantage of his opponent's inertia, he spent more than a month after Sharpsburg in replenishing, refreshing, and drilling the Army of Northern Virginia for further action. When McClellan in late October crossed the Potomac into Virginia, Lee again split his forces, sending Jackson into the Shenandoah Valley and holding Longstreet and Stuart east of the Blue Ridge, thus always keeping one wing in front of the enemy and leaving the other free to maneuver, to strike his opponent's line of communications or to threaten Washington with seizure if the Federal army should venture too far from base.

Upon learning in early November that McClellan had been replaced by General Ambrose E. Burnside, Lee remarked with a touch of whimsy, "We [McClellan and I] always understood each other so well. I fear they may continue to make these changes till they find some one whom I don't understand." He soon understood Burnside, understood with apparent intuition that he intended to cross the lower Rappahannock River and drive straight for Richmond. As the Federal army began to concentrate on the north side of the river opposite Fredericksburg, Lee moved Longstreet into position along a dominating ridge behind the town and ordered Jackson there from the Valley. By December 10 the entire Army of Northern Virginia, now seventy-eight thousand strong, was assembled for the coming attack, which Lee resolved to meet point-blank.

For two days Lee's snipers delayed the bridging of the Rappahannock by the Union engineers, but by nightfall of December 12 Burnside's army of some 120 thousand was south of the river and the battle of Fredericksburg was ready to begin. From dawn until dark of the thirteenth Lee sat at his observation post on the hill that has ever since borne his name and watched the blue-clad columns hurl themselves repeatedly and futilely against his positions. The slaughter among the attackers was severe, especially in front of Longstreet's position along Marye's Heights on the left wing of the Confederate line, where the main Union effort was directed. Fredericksburg was one of Lee's cheapest victories: his army suffered only 5,300 casualties while inflicting some 12,600 casualties on the Federals.

Here Lee revealed for an instant the man of war at the core of the man of chivalry and piety. At one point in the battle, as Jackson's line repulsed an enemy assault, Lee was heard to say, "It is well that war is so terrible—we should grow too fond of it."

Anticipating a renewal of the attack the following day, Lee prepared his lines to deliver a final punishing repulse, after which he hoped to launch a counterattack that would further cripple the Federal army, perhaps destroy it. He was denied this opportunity; the morning of the fourteenth he found the enemy in a defensive formation protected by their superior artillery positioned on the heights across the river. For two days the armies lay facing each other in this fashion. Then, during the night of the fifteenth, Burnside withdrew north of the Rappahannock to seek another approach to Richmond.

Lee has been criticized for failing to counterattack his beaten and demoralized foe during the night following the battle. Possibly he lost a favorable occasion to do so. Yet the probability of success in such an operation was highly questionable, and certainly he was wise not to attack after the Federals had assumed the defensive.

While the opposing forces in Virginia nursed their wounds from Fredericksburg and gathered strength for the coming campaigns, Lee's attention was directed to other theaters of the war. Largely through his generalship, the most formidable of the Union efforts to overwhelm the Confederacy, the drives for Richmond, had been beaten. But west of the Appalachians the southern lines were dangerously bent and pierced. General U. S. Grant was preparing a move against Vicksburg, the major Confederate position on the Mississippi River, and a strong Union army under General

Rosecrans was lodged in central Tennessee, poised to march against Chattanooga, a vital rail center, the gateway to Georgia and the lower southeast. As various southern military and civil leaders called for a transfer of troops from Virginia to strengthen the faltering Confederate armies in the West, President Davis appealed to Lee for advice.

Lee agreed that a shift of troops to the West would be wise if it could be done expeditiously and if the situation in Virginia would permit it. He had been contemplating the idea of sending a strong contingent of his army to Tennessee, he said. But he reminded the president that the Confederacy lacked the transport facilities to match the Federals in moving great bodies of troops and their arms and equipment over wide distances, and he cautioned that as long as a powerful Union force remained intact in northern Virginia such a move could be made only by exposing Richmond and the entire eastern theater to immediate invasion. When in early April 1863 Confederate Secretary of War James A. Seddon requested a division of Lee's army to reinforce the Confederate army opposing Rosecrans, Lee replied by recommending an alternative strategy that he felt would neutralize the Federal threat in the West and at the same time protect Richmond and the East.

He urged that the major Confederate armies in both the East and the West be strengthened with troops drawn from the relatively idle departments of the south Atlantic and Gulf coasts. Then, said Lee, these reinforced armies—Joseph E. Johnston's in Mississippi, Braxton Bragg's in Tennessee, and his own in Virginia—ought to seize the initiative in their respective sectors. Johnston ought to concentrate his forces and attack Grant; Bragg ought to advance into Kentucky; and Lee should strike north again in order to menace Washington and the cities of the East. "The readiest method of relieving pressure upon General Johnston," he said, "is for the [Army of Northern Virginia] to cross into Maryland. . . . [Also] greater relief would in this way be afforded to the armies in

Tennessee." This plan followed a principle that would have been recognizable to the famed German military theorist Karl von Clausewitz, who had written that at every opportunity one ought to threaten the enemy's territory with the "flashing sword of vengeance."

Meantime, Lee searched the portents for a hint of the enemy's intention on his own front. His warning that the powerful Union army in Virginia, now numbering 130 thousand, would not lie idle while he dispatched troops to faraway Tennessee was soon fulfilled. He now had a fresh opponent before him, Major General Joseph Hooker, a confident and aggressive soldier who had proclaimed, "I have the finest army the sun ever shone on. My plans are perfect. May God have mercy on General Lee, for I will have none."

In late April Hooker put the Army of the Potomac in motion. His plan was bold and ingenious; it was quite similar to Lee's operations at Second Manassas. Leaving one force of forty thousand under General John Sedgwick facing Lee at Fredericksburg, Hooker with the main body of his force swung twenty miles to the west, crossed the Rappahannock and its tributary, the Rapidan, and moved through a heavily wooded area known as the Wilderness to strike Lee from the rear or turn him out of his strong position on the heights and destroy him in the open.

Lee did not sit and wait to be destroyed. Promptly discerning his opponent's purpose, he adopted a countermeasure that was even bolder than Hooker's design. Two Confederate divisions under Longstreet were absent, having been sent at President Davis's urging to defend Richmond and its rail lines against a threatened Federal advance from the coast and to collect desperately needed provisions from eastern North Carolina. Despite this potential handicap, Lee proposed to parry Sedgwick at Fredericksburg with a single division under General Jubal Early while he engaged Hooker's main body with the remaining forty-three thousand troops of the Army of Northern Virginia. Screening his action with Stuart's cavalry, Lee moved his force to a position on the turnpike three miles east of Chancellorsville, a single structure located at a crossroads in the Wilderness, and there on May 1 engaged the advancing Federal columns. Surprised and stunned by Lee's audacity and self-confidence, Hooker recoiled to Chancellorsville and placed his army on the defensive. Lee sensed that he now held the initiative.

That evening, after receiving word from his cavalry that the Union right flank was "in the air" [exposed], Lee met with Jackson in the woods, where the two of them designed one of the boldest tactical actions in modern warfare. Seated on cracker-boxes by a flickering campfire, they planned a movement by Jackson to envelop the open enemy flank, something of a repetition of Second Manassas. Jackson proposed to take with him his entire command of twenty-eight thousand troops, leaving Lee with only fourteen thousand to face the overwhelming Federal numbers throughout most of the following day. Startled at first, Lee reflected for a moment, then said, "Well. Go on."

Jackson marched at dawn of May 2, and shortly after five o'clock that afternoon struck Hooker's vulnerable flank like a tidal wave. Taken by complete surprise, with arms stacked and suppers cooking over their campfires, the Union troops there broke in panic. Jackson pressed on, rolling up the enemy line as he advanced, determined to sever Hooker's communications with his base on the Rappahannock. After dark the fighting subsided. Seeking to complete the victory the following day, Jackson rode forward for a personal reconnaissance of the terrain and situation.

Lee soon received word that dulled his anticipation of success. Awakened at 2:30 in the morning to be given an account of Jackson's operations of the previous day, he was told also that his peerless lieutenant had been wounded by his own troops at the very moment of success. "Ah captain," Lee said to the message bearer, "any victory is dearly bought which deprives us of the services of General Jackson, even for a short time." Then Lee issued orders for renewing the attack the following morning, and for uniting the two wings of the army. "It is necessary that the glorious victory thus far achieved be prosecuted with the utmost vigor, and the enemy given no time to rally."

Reopening the battle at dawn, Lee soon achieved the desired junction of his assault lines and pressed purposefully toward the Rappahannock as Hooker's forces yielded ground before him. Sensing the beginning of a rout that might enable him to destroy his foe, Lee rode forward to direct his pursuit and preserve the momentum of victory. His presence at the front ignited the spirit of his troops and set off a wild ovation in his favor. As described by a staff officer, "I thought it must have been from such scenes as this that men in ancient days ascended to the dignity of gods."

His hour of exultation was cut short by the receipt of two messages of grave import. The first brought tears to his eyes and a choking sound in his voice: Jackson's surgeon had been obliged to amputate the wounded arm. The second dispatch was, for the moment, even more alarming: Union forces under Sedgwick had crossed the river at Fredericksburg, had driven Early from Marye's Heights, and were now marching to strike Lee from the rear.

Cool in the midst of apparent disaster, Lee quickly improvised a plan for the emergency. Sending a single division to check Sedgwick, and gambling that Hooker would remain passive, Lee left half of his army under Stuart (Hill also had been wounded) and hastened with the other half to attack Sedgwick in the hope of destroying him. Lee's bold action removed the threat to his rear, but he was unable to achieve his aim of destroying Sedgwick, who fought a skillful delaying action and escaped across the river.

With Early's strengthened command again holding Marye's Heights, Lee shuttled the remainder of his reserves back to

Chancellorsville, hoping even yet to strike Hooker south of the river. By nightfall of the fifth the weary and battle-marked Confederates were in position: Lee ordered an attack for the following dawn. But dawn found the Federal lines empty; Hooker had recrossed the river during the night.

Lee's disappointment over failing to destroy the Union army was keen. Still, Chancellorsville was a brilliant victory. He had inflicted almost seventeen thousand casualties upon the enemy while suffering fewer than thirteen thousand casualties in his own forces. He had defeated in open battle an opponent with more than twice his numbers, and had wrecked the most determined Federal campaign yet launched against the nerve center of the Confederacy. A plantation girl in faraway Texas spoke for a multitude of southerners when she called him "Lee the invincible."

The guns of Chancellorsville had scarcely grown silent when Lee received the message that he had prayed would not come. Jackson was dead. Lee knew precisely and acknowledged freely how much he owed to his great subordinate for his brightest victories. To Jackson himself he had written at the climax of the recent engagement, "I congratulate you upon the victory, which is due to your skill and energy." To Jackson's chaplain he had said movingly, "He has lost his left arm, but I have lost my right."

To his troops Lee now issued a proclamation: "But while we mourn his death, we feel that his spirit still lives, and will inspire the whole army with his indomitable courage and unshaken confidence in God as our hope and our strength. . . . Let officers and men emulate his invincible determination to do everything in the defense of our beloved country." To a friend Lee later said, "Such an executive officer the sun never shone on. . . . Straight as the needle to the pole he advanced to the execution of my purpose." Lee also confided, "Any victory would be dear at such a price. I know not how to replace him." Lee was right. The Army of Northern Virginia was never the same again.

Lee's electrifying victory gave the Confederate authorities an opportunity to reevaluate their entire strategic situation. Virginia was temporarily safe, but the Confederate lines in the West were on the point of collapse. Even as the battle of Chancellorsville was raging, General U. S. Grant successfully crossed his army to the east bank of the Mississippi River south of Vicksburg and was now moving resolutely in his campaign against the city. In central Tennessee General Rosecrans was preparing to open a drive against Bragg's army in the move for Chattanooga.

Confederate Secretary of War Seddon now renewed his recommendation for a transfer of troops from Lee's army to the West in order to strengthen the defenses of Vicksburg. Again Lee opposed such a move, and this time he elaborated somewhat on his reasons, saying, "It is a question between Virginia and the Mississippi." Also, "The distance and the uncertainty of the employment of the troops [in the West] are unfavorable."

Lee's references to Virginia versus the Mississippi and to the problem of distance are quite clear and understandable. Moving a large body of troops and all their armaments and equipment to the West by the limping Confederate rail system was the equivalent of moving an army across Siberia today. Lee's reference to the unfavorable employment of the troops was a coded way of saying that he had little faith in the ability of the generals in the West to put the troops to their most effective use, and that he believed he could do more with an intact Army of Northern Virginia than they could do with a composite force hastily assembled from throughout the South. When Davis learned of Lee's reply he said it was what he had anticipated and that he concurred with Lee.

The deliberations on Confederate strategy came to a head in mid-May. Lee left his army in the field and went by train to Richmond to present his views in person. There, according to the War Department clerk and diarist, John B. Jones, Lee was closeted for a long period with Davis and Seddon. Unfortunately, no record remains of what was said in this conference, other than an account written years later by Postmaster General John Reagan describing Davis's briefing of the entire cabinet after meeting with Lee. But from Lee's previous statements and Reagan's account of the cabinet meeting, and from the events that began shortly to unfold, one may fairly conclude that Lee emphasized and augmented all the reasons he had already given for favoring a course of action other than sending a part of his army west. Both Davis and Seddon were convinced. The Gettysburg campaign was the result.

Lee intended his invasion of the North to be the main effort in a larger strategy on behalf of the Confederacy, a strategy that would enable his army to feed on enemy supplies, draw the Union army out of Virginia, relieve the pressure on Vicksburg and Chattanooga, and at the same time convince the northern population that the Confederacy was unconquerable and the Union ought therefore to accept an end to hostilities. He had written to his wife a few weeks earlier, saying he believed that if the Confederates could "baffle" the Federals a few months longer, the northern people would reject the Republicans in the 1864 elections and replace them with an administration dedicated to making peace.

Lee fully realized that the South was not strong enough to conquer the North or destroy its ability to make war. On the contrary, he reasoned that despite the Confederacy's recent victories in the field, it was growing relatively weaker with every battle. As his columns moved north he wrote to Davis, "We should not . . . conceal from ourselves that our resources in men are constantly diminishing, and the disproportion in this respect between us and our enemies . . . is steadily augmenting." He was aware that the South's best hope for winning independence was by stifling the northern will to continue the war. This could be done, he felt, by a combination of paralyzing Confederate military successes and astute Confederate statecraft.

His bid for diplomatic support of the military effort was made in a suggestion to President Davis that the Confederate invasion of the North be accompanied by a peace overture on the part of the Confederate government. Lee cautioned against an unconditional demand for southern independence and advised Davis to permit the northern population to believe that the Union might be restored through negotiation once a truce was adopted. Lee reasoned that if hostilities should cease, they probably would never be resumed, and the Confederacy would achieve its goal through northern default.

Obviously, this proposal contained an element of deception, as many political and diplomatic overtures and all military strategies do. Both Davis and Lincoln at times resorted to such deceptions, and Lee was a master of deception in the field. But he was a novice in both politics and diplomacy, and he found it difficult to separate public ethics from personal morality. In offering his advice to Davis, he insisted that all steps taken should be "honorable" and done "consistently with truth," by which he apparently intended to make clear that he was willing to withhold information but unwilling to issue an explicit falsehood.

He possibly was wrong in assuming that the North would not have taken up arms again if the Union could not have been preserved at the conference table. But he was right in believing that the South's only hope lay in a collapse of the northern will, in urging a blow at northern morale, and in advising against the premature announcement of inflexible southern peace terms. Many citizens of the North now considered the war effort futile and yearned for peace.

Lee's campaign began in early June with a movement into the lower Shenandoah Valley. The Army of Northern Virginia, with a strength of seventy-five thousand, was now organized into three infantry corps—the First Corps under Longstreet, the Second Corps under Lieutenant General Richard Ewell, and the

Third Corps under Lieutenant General A. P. Hill—plus Lieutenant General Stuart's cavalry. Leaving Hill temporarily to preoccupy the Federals at Fredericksburg, and screening his move with Stuart's cavalry, Lee was a week on the march before his opponent became aware of it. Not until the thirteenth did Hooker begin to shift his forces to meet the Confederate move. Two days later Lee's advance corps (Ewell's) began crossing the Potomac near Shepherdstown in West Virginia.

As Lee marched north he sought to devise measures that would strengthen his own blow and weaken the enemy's defense. He repeated his earlier requests for reinforcements from the Richmond defenses and the lower Atlantic coast, urging Davis to reduce the garrisons there to mere token forces, and he recommended that General Beauregard be brought with these reserves to northern Virginia in order to make a feint in the direction of Washington to divert a part of Hooker's army to the protection of the national capital from the south. A mere "army in effigy" under Beauregard would have good effect, said Lee. "His presence would give magnitude to even a small demonstration and tend greatly to perplex and confound the enemy."

As Ewell's corps moved across the corner of Maryland toward Pennsylvania, Lee hastened Longstreet and Hill after him, while Stuart's cavalry secured the passes of the Blue Ridge and guarded the eastern flank and rear of the elongated column. Once across the Potomac the Confederate line of march lay west of, and was shielded by, South Mountain and its northward extension, which actually constituted a continuation of the Blue Ridge north of the river. Drawing upon his experience with General Scott in Mexico, Lee determined to abandon his line of communication and, for the moment, live by foraging on the enemy territory. By June 28, the entire Army of Northern Virginia, except for Stuart, was in Pennsylvania.

Foraging required the seizure of supplies, especially food, from the civilian population of the enemy. Keenly aware of the potential for vandalism and rapine, and seeking to control soldiers who were both famished and hot with a desire for vengeance because of what they had witnessed on their own soil, Lee issued a remarkable order against pillage, invoking the obligations of civilization and Christianity and warning that such misconduct would offend "Him to whom vengeance belongeth, without whose favor and support our efforts must all prove in vain." His foragers were ordered to pay with receipts redeemable by the Confederate government for the goods they took.

Among the seizures carried out by Longstreet's cavalry were a number of black residents, some of them escaped slaves, the rest free persons. There is no evidence that Lee knew about these seizures; he unquestionably had enough on his mind without being concerned with such matters. If he knew that any blacks were taken, he probably was under the impression that all of them were runaways and thus, under the legalities prevailing on the eve of the war, had been subject to arrest and return to their owners. The seizure of free blacks, except for reasons of military security, would have violated both Lee's own concept of morality and the practices of the state of Virginia, where some fifty-eight thousand free blacks resided. It is extremely doubtful that he would have countenanced such an action.

Notwithstanding the skill with which Lee deceived and out-maneuvered his opponent in gaining northern soil, the campaign was, from the beginning, beset with miscarriages. On June 9 while holding a review of his troops at Brandy Station in Virginia, Stuart was surprised by a powerful Union cavalry force, and though he finally repelled the attack, he allowed his headquarters to be captured in the fray, including some papers that may have alerted the Union command to a Confederate movement.

Lee's request for reinforcements and for a diversion threatening Washington from the south went unfulfilled. Most of the reserves from the lower Atlantic coast had by now been sent west, and Davis was too apprehensive of an attack on Richmond from the peninsula to be willing to send troops to Lee from the Richmond garrison or from nearby North Carolina. The president made no effort to bring up Beauregard or to create an army in effigy. Lee's ideas for perplexing and confounding the enemy came to naught.

Moreover, since crossing the Potomac, Lee had lost touch with Stuart, whose reconnaissances had been of decisive value in the past and in whom Lee placed great faith. Lee had ordered the cavalry leader to keep contact with Ewell's right flank, gather supplies, and collect information on the enemy as the Confederates advanced. But Lee, as usual, had also given Stuart discretionary authority to attempt a swing around the Union army with the object of disrupting its communications as much as possible. Stuart, determined, according to some students of the campaign, to assuage his chagrin over the Brandy Station affair, had ridden away on a sweeping raid in the direction of Washington, then north to encircle the enemy force. Lee now urgently needed information; he was quoted as saying in frustration, "I do not know what to do; I cannot hear from General Stuart, the eye of the army." Also, when Stuart joined him in the midst of the forthcoming battle, "Well, General Stuart, you are here at last": coming from Lee, a sharp rebuke.

On or about June 28 he learned from an informer that the opposing force was north of the Potomac and located in the vicinity of Frederick, Maryland, only about thirty-five miles south and east of Lee's headquarters in Chambersburg, Pennsylvania. He learned also that Hooker had been replaced by Major General George G. Meade, one of Lee's comrades of the Mexican War. Lee was quoted as saying when he received this information, "[He] will commit no blunder in my front, and if I make one he will make haste to take advantage of it." This was a remarkably perceptive appraisal of his new opponent.

Sensing, perhaps, both danger and opportunity, Lee at once

began to concentrate his infantry corps in and about the village of Cashtown. From here a Confederate brigade from Hill's corps was dispatched the afternoon of June 30 to nearby Gettysburg for the purpose of taking a supply of Union army shoes said to be stored there. Two miles west of their objective the Confederates were halted by fire from Federal cavalry. That night Hill authorized for the following morning a movement into town by an entire division. The battle of Gettysburg was about to begin.

Lee was initially reluctant to undertake a major engagement with the enemy at this time and place. He had hoped to be able to accomplish the object of his northern offensive without such a battle, but he had also written Secretary Seddon that he was determined to seize any favorable opportunity to "assail" the Union army and, as quoted by a subordinate, "virtually destroy [it]." Lee had not ordered the attack at Gettysburg; it had simply developed out of a meeting of the two forces. He was aware that his ranking subordinate, Longstreet, opposed an attack and preferred maneuvering in an effort to induce Meade to assault the Confederates in a defensive position of their own choosing. But after arriving on the field that afternoon and watching his troops advance successfully, Lee changed his mind. Convinced that his own concentration was more nearly completed than his opponent's, he made the fateful decision to attack the enemy without delay.

Gettysburg was almost Lee's undoing. To win the battle he had to overcome an army approximately fifteen thousand men stronger than his own that held the commanding terrain of the area: Cemetery Hill lying south of the town; Cemetery Ridge, which extended southward from Cemetery Hill; and Little Round Top, a hill overlooking the southern end of Cemetery Ridge. The main effort of the initial attack, delivered in the afternoon of July 1 before all of either army was on the field, was made by Ewell from the north and through the town of Gettysburg. Lee, seeing at a glance the importance of Cemetery Hill, ordered Ewell to seize it "if practicable, but to avoid a general engagement." Partly through the optional nature of Lee's order, and partly through Ewell's hesitancy, the mission was not attempted.

Lee then purposed, over Longstreet's objection, to continue the battle the following day with an enveloping attack by Longstreet's corps against what Lee believed to be the south flank of the Union line on Cemetery Ridge. Delivered during the late afternoon, the attack was formidable, but because the Union force actually was not deployed as Lee's reconnaissance troops had indicated, the Confederates found themselves drawn into a contest for the possession of Little Round Top and the lower end of Cemetery Ridge. Fiercely opposed by superior numbers, and only erratically supported by the two corps of Hill and Ewell, the attack eventually failed.

Thwarted in his attempts to seize the strategic heights at the extremities of the Union line, Lee now resolved to strike a final blow with troops drawn from the corps of Longstreet and Hill, with Longstreet in command, against the enemy center on Cemetery Ridge. Ewell and Hill, with the remainder of his corps, were to make supporting attacks. Again Longstreet demurred, renewing his insistence upon a turning movement around the Union left to draw the opposing army into a battle on ground more advantageous to the Confederates. Unmoved by these arguments, Lee ordered the frontal assault, and Longstreet sullenly acquiesced.

By one o'clock in the afternoon of July 3, the stage was set for the final act in the drama of Gettysburg. The opposing lines faced each other from the crests of parallel ridges, the Confederates on Seminary Ridge and the Federals on Cemetery Ridge, approximately a mile apart. Shortly after the hour the Confederate artillery opened with more than one hundred guns; the Federal batteries promptly took up the challenge. For almost an hour the duel continued, then, one by one, many of the Federal guns ceased firing, apparently silenced by the Confederate fire. Upon Longstreet's reluctant signal the assault force of 12,500 to 13,000 troops led by Major General George E. Pickett, Brigadier General J. Johnston Pettigrew, and Major General Isaac R. Trimble moved forward. Dressed in line, with colors flashing in the summer sunlight, the Confederate infantry advanced against Cemetery Ridge.

Cemetery Ridge wore a fitting name. Many of the Federal cannons along the top, having earlier stopped their firing as a ruse to deceive the Confederates, now opened with a cannonade that tore great gaps in the approaching ranks and littered the ground with the fallen. Yet the dwindling attackers moved on, seemingly oblivious of the carnage. When they came within rifle range of the enemy position, the waiting Federal infantry opened fire with a deadly fusillade. Onward still pressed the remnants of the assaulting formation until a dauntless handful gained the objective and struggled face to face with the Federal infantry and with artillerists at their pieces. But to no avail. The Confederates were too few to hold their ground. Soon the survivors were drifting back across the smoking fields, and the battle of Gettysburg was over.

Why was Lee defeated in this greatest of Civil War encounters? Was it because Ewell proved irresolute and lost favorable occasions to seize Cemetery Hill on the first two days or Culp's Hill, which overlooked Cemetery Hill from the east, on the second and third days? Or because Longstreet sulked and dawdled on the second and third days, and threw away opportunities when prompt and positive obedience of orders might have smashed the Federals before they were firmly in position? Would "Mighty Stonewall" have accomplished here what lesser men could not do? All of these explanations and speculations have been offered.

Yet, whatever mistakes and shortcomings the subordinates may have been guilty of, Lee himself must bear the ultimate responsibility for his defeat. If his army was indeed capable of winning at Gettysburg, then he ought to have issued and enforced the orders required to achieve the victory. If, on the other hand, his army was not capable of winning there, then he erred in risking it against so strong a position. Whatever the cause of his repulse, he unquestionably overestimated the ability of flesh and blood to prevail over fire and iron. According to his own testimony, he had come to believe his men "invincible."

Possibly his decisions to attack at Gettysburg, and especially the decision for the ill-fated action on the third day, were simply products of his own combativeness and willingness to take the big risk. These decisions may have marked a reassertion of an inherent trait to deliver frontal assaults when everything else had failed to accomplish what he wanted: the trait that had launched the attack on Malvern Hill at the end of the peninsular campaign.

Other speculations come to mind. Notwithstanding the earlier action, Lee's frontal assaults at Gettysburg violated his own tactical doctrine, which he had once written explicitly to Jackson, instructing him to avoid attacks against an enemy in position, and instead to conserve his troops by turning the enemy out of position. Lee had won his greatest offensive victories, Second Manassas and Chancellorsville, employing the kind of tactics he recommended to Jackson. A distinguished scholar on Civil War command and strategy, Archer Jones, says Lee's mode at Gettysburg was an "aberration" from his usual procedure.

Besides his decisions to make frontal assaults at Gettysburg, Lee seemed not himself during the engagement. The Lee of Second Manassas, Antietam, or Chancellorsville is scarcely recognizable at Gettysburg. His orders here, most of them given only orally, were tardy, fragmentary, tentative, and ambiguous, radically so in comparison with those of the earlier battles. Throughout the critical fighting of Longstreet's attack on the afternoon of the second day Lee was extremely inert; he was said to have sat placidly on a stump, receiving only one report and sending only one message. Freeman says the Army of Northern Virginia was actually without a commander that day.

This behavior suggests severe physical and mental exhaustion. For two years he had lived under constant pressure of the most taxing nature imaginable. During the previous year his army had been engaged in five campaigns against immensely superior forces. In each campaign, Lee, like the commander of the British fleet in the first World War, was the one man capable of losing the war in an afternoon. The condition of Lee's health also suggests exhaustion. Early in the previous spring he had experienced what is now believed to have been a heart attack; and at Gettysburg he sustained an onset of the commonest of Civil War maladies, diarrhea. His mind during that engagement may have been clouded by illness and campaign fatigue.*

But Lee was never greater than in the hours of peril immediately after his broken lines fell back from Cemetery Ridge. Weakened by a horde of casualties, virtually out of ammunition, facing a triumphant foe who was being steadily reinforced, and lodged deep in hostile territory with a major river between there and home, his army hung on the edge of disaster. Shaking off his lethargy, Lee was everywhere, riding among the grimy, stunned soldiers, encouraging them to bind up wounds, pick up fallen muskets, and take positions for defense. He shouldered the full responsibility for the defeat, saying to one brigadier general who was overwhelmed with the sense of loss and failure, "Never mind, general, all this has been my fault—it is I that have lost this fight, and you must help me out of it the best way you can."

---

* An episode in World War II illustrates pointedly the effects of exhaustion on a commander's power of decision. After the great battle of the Ardennes in the winter of 1944–45, Gen. Dwight D. Eisenhower became so exhausted that he was unable to think clearly. Only after a vacation of several days on the French Riviera was he able to resume his duties.

Throughout the remainder of the afternoon and into the night he labored to brace his army against an expected counterattack and prepare it for the inevitable retreat to Virginia. Not until long past midnight did he ride, preoccupied and weary, through his slumbering bivouacs and into his headquarters. Only then did he yield to his feelings with the exclamation, "Too bad! Oh, too bad!"

The retreat from Gettysburg was a nightmare of hunger, fatigue, anxiety, and agony, as the defeated column slogged back through rain and mud, and the long wagon train of wounded bumped mercilessly along the roads leading south. On July 6 Lee reached the Potomac at Williamsport, Maryland, only to find the river unbridged and unfordable there. His worst fears of Federal pursuit and attack seemed on the point of coming true. But Meade followed cautiously; Lee's defensive dispositions were masterful; the Confederate engineers succeeded in improvising a pontoon bridge to cross the trains; and fords were located to accommodate the infantry. By the fourteenth Lee had the Army of Northern Virginia, thinned by twenty-eight thousand casualties but still intact in formation and formidable in spirit and combat power, back on southern soil.

Defeat and Surrender

Gettysburg left its mark on Lee. Fearing that defeat had weakened him in the eyes of the public, and possibly of the army also, he reasoned that his leadership was inevitably impaired and that he ought therefore to step aside in favor of a successor who held the confidence of both the people and the troops. In late July he wrote Davis asking to be replaced by a "younger and abler" man. Davis at once affirmed his steadfast faith in Lee, saying that this confidence was shared by all the "reflecting men of the country" and that finding an abler man anywhere would be impossible. Lee must remain in command, urged the president, and Lee accepted this decision without a further word.

He spent the rest of the summer rebuilding his army in its defensive position behind the Rapidan River. Warily he observed Meade's deliberate advance into northern Virginia, hoping for a misstep that would enable him to deliver a crippling counterblow. But the outcome of the Gettysburg campaign had eroded Lee's opposition to the plan for sending a portion of his army west of the Appalachians, and when in early September Davis expressed a desire to reinforce Bragg, who had fallen back to Chattanooga and was at the point of losing that city, Lee acquiesced and ordered Longstreet there temporarily with twelve thousand troops.

Bragg's victory in the battle of Chickamauga (September 19–20) seemed to justify the decision. Immediately upon learning of what was reported to be a decisive Confederate triumph there, Lee suggested that Longstreet, in returning to Virginia, strike a blow at a Union force under Burnside that had taken Knoxville. But the early reports of a decisive Confederate victory at Chickamauga soon proved illusory. What Lincoln later said of Rosecrans after the battle, that he was stunned and acting like a duck that had been hit on the head, could have been said of Bragg during the battle. He faltered at the moment of victory and squandered what may have been an opportunity to destroy the Union army.

Longstreet now had an occasion to evaluate Lee's generalship in the light of his experience with Bragg. Shortly after Chickamauga Longstreet wrote the secretary of war, saying: "I am convinced that nothing but the hand of God can save us or help as long as we have our present commander. . . . Can't you send us General Lee? The army in Virginia can operate defensively, while our operations here should be offensive—until we recover Tennessee at all events. We need some great mind as General Lee's (nothing more) to accomplish this."

Eventually, after weeks of waging a futile siege of the Union army at Chattanooga, and while that army was being heavily reinforced in preparation for renewing the Union offensive, Bragg dispatched Longstreet to Knoxville, where he engaged in a siege that was as unproductive as Bragg's at Chattanooga. In late November, partly as a result of this weakening of the main army, Bragg suffered a disastrous defeat at Missionary Ridge overlooking Chattanooga. Collectively, the operations beginning with Chickamauga cost the Confederacy far more than it had gained by the transfer of forces from Virginia to Tennessee. Lee had been right in questioning the ability of the western generals to use his troops effectively.

Meanwhile, Lee was not idle. Upon learning that Meade had sent reinforcements to bolster the Federal army at Chattanooga, Lee resolved to seize the initiative in the East once again. Crossing the Rapidan and Rappahannock, he attempted to turn Meade's right flank as he had turned Pope's flank at Second Manassas more than two years before. But Hill attacked prematurely at Bristoe Station (October 14) and was repulsed with sharp losses, thus permitting Meade to withdraw in good order and entrench his army behind Bull Run. Lee wisely declined to risk an assault on this strong position and instead retired behind the Rapidan. Meade then advanced against him and attempted a turning movement around the Confederate right, but he halted when he found Lee's army facing east and strongly positioned behind a stream known as the Mine Run. Lee at once launched a countermovement to turn Meade's flank but on December 2 discovered the Federals withdrawing across the Rapidan. This ended the major operations in Virginia for the winter.

The break in fighting gave Lee an opportunity to pause and survey the military situation of the Confederacy as a whole. What he observed was grim. The entire line of the Mississippi River was now lost, thus denying the Confederacy the resources of the vast area west of that waterway, and the city of Chattanooga, the portal to the southeast, was in the hands of the enemy.

Lee did something that was rare for him—he volunteered advice to Davis, saying that the Federal army at Chattanooga menaced the entire state of Georgia with its factories and provisions, and that the forthcoming invasion of that state must be stopped if the Confederacy was to survive. Let the Confederate army there be reinforced from the scattered garrisons along the lower Atlantic and Gulf coasts, he urged, and place Beauregard in command.

As for the security of the coastal areas if their defenses should be weakened, he reasoned, "Upon the defence of the country threatened by [the enemy advance] depends the safety of the points now held by us on the Atlantic." His was a prophetic warning and timely advice, but it came to naught.

Lee's admonition occurred at that critical point in the course of the war when President Abraham Lincoln was about to appoint Ulysses S. Grant to the position of general in chief of all Union armies, with full authority to employ them as he saw fit in a unified effort against the Confederacy. The Confederate military forces urgently needed a comparable unity of command and strategy, for a significant portion of the South's fighting efficiency was being wasted by a futile dispersion of troops and a want of proper coordination in their use.

Lee was aware of the need, but he also recognized that Davis opposed any thought of delegating the supreme military command to a subordinate. Lee's deep sense of respect for civilian authority sealed his lips on the matter. His advice in favor of a concentration of forces to defend the state of Georgia was as near as he could bring himself to offering a candid criticism of the administration's military policy.

When spring came Lee found himself confronting his ultimate test of skill and will. His new opponent in northern Virginia was Grant, for though Meade remained technically in command of the Army of the Potomac, Grant accompanied this army, provided the overall direction to its operations, and, more important, generated the strength of will in top command that it had always lacked.

On May 4 Lee learned that Grant was marching the Union army, some 120 thousand strong, southward across the Rapidan and into the dense woods of the Wilderness, the site of the Chancellorsville battlefield. Lee's army was again united; Longstreet and his troops had recently returned from Tennessee, bringing Lee's total strength up to about 61 thousand. Determined to gain the

initiative and take his opponent at the greatest possible dis-
advantage—that is, while on the move through the kind of area
that would partially nullify the Federal superiority in numbers
and artillery—Lee ordered an immediate attack.

For two days (May 5–6) the battle of the Wilderness raged, as
Lee struck frontally with a part of his troops and, at the same time,
attempted to press Longstreet's corps plus one of Hill's divisions
around the Union left flank to repeat the victorious tactics of
Chancellorsville. Driving in both Union flanks, Lee punished the
Union army severely, inflicting some 18,000 casualties while
sustaining only 10,800.

Unlike Pope or Hooker before him, Grant refused to withdraw
when he appeared to have been beaten. Instead, he broke off
action and marched east and south, with the object of turning Lee's
right flank. Sensing his opponent's purpose and tenacity, Lee
ordered a direct road cut through the woods to Spotsylvania Court
House and shifted his lines there to intercept Grant's movement.

Lee's failure to halt Grant in the Wilderness opened a new
phase in Lee's generalship. Although he was a firm believer in
the attack as the surest means of defense and would continue to
seek favorable occasions to strike Grant, he now recognized that
he lacked sufficient strength to mount a general offensive as long
as his foe was willing to absorb heavy casualties and maintain
the full pressure of his greater numbers. Lee turned, therefore,
to a strategy of conservation of force, waging skillful defensive
warfare to safeguard his own resources while consuming those
of his adversary. Possibly in this way he could still exhaust the
northern will for victory.

Beginning on May 8 Lee engaged Grant's forces at Spotsylvania
Court House for twelve days of intermittent but bitter combat.
Fighting from an inverted V formation, the entrenched Confederates defeated every Union attack, though on one occasion a
massed assault temporarily penetrated the apex of the southern

line, a sector that had already earned the name "Bloody Angle." Again, Lee inflicted a dreadful number of casualties, 18,000 Union to 9,500 Confederate. When on the morning of the twenty-first Lee learned that Grant was again drawing away from his front and sideslipping around his right flank, Lee at once selected another point of interception, the North Anna River.

Marching rapidly south along the chord of Grant's arc, Lee reached his destination in a single day and night. Arranging his troops on the south side of the stream, he drew Grant into a cunningly devised trap that gave the Confederates an opportunity to attack and destroy or cripple a portion of the Union army while the entire force was separated into three parts by the river. But Lee was unable to spring the trap because of a violent intestinal upset that confined him to his tent during the critical period of May 24 and 25. Grant promptly withdrew and again swung east and south in an effort to work his way around the living barrier. Lee once again anticipated his opponent's object and moved effectively to block it. During the closing days of May he shifted by stages to the right and rear, always extending his line just in time to protect his flank against being turned.

By early June Lee's right was anchored on the Chickahominy River only nine miles east of Richmond. His army was intact, strengthened by troops drawn from Confederate forces that had won recent victories below the James River and at New Market in the Shenandoah Valley. Lee's position was favorable and his communications with Richmond secure. Grant now despaired of taking Lee by maneuver and on June 3 rammed his army directly into the fortified southern line in the battle of Cold Harbor. It was a repetition of Fredericksburg on a reduced scale, a repulse of the Federals that cost Grant more than seven thousand casualties in less than an hour, while the Confederate dead and wounded amounted to fifteen hundred. That evening Lee wrote President Davis, "Our loss today has been small, and our success, under the blessing of

God, all that we could expect." He could not know that Cold Harbor would be his last military victory.

Lee's generalship from the Wilderness through Cold Harbor offers a remarkable lesson in the conduct of defensive operations. His capacity to read the intentions of his opponents and his skill in moving to checkmate them became a theme of admiration to foe and friend alike. A soldier in Grant's army wrote in his diary that Lee must be a great strategist, because everywhere the Union army went, the rebels were already there. Lee's employment of field fortifications was superb; he made the pick and spade indispensable adjuncts of the musket and cannon.

Lee's skill exacted from the Federals a fearful toll in dead and wounded. In the operations beginning in the Wilderness and ending with Cold Harbor, he had inflicted over fifty-five thousand casualties on the enemy, a number almost equal to the initial strength of his own army. In spite of the tremendous exertions and sacrifices of the Army of the Potomac, it was still farther from Richmond than McClellan's army had been in the summer of 1862. The Confederates appeared to be invincible. An English student of the American Civil War, Sir Frederic Maurice, wrote later of Lee's conduct of this campaign, "[It] is a classical example in military history of how these objects [conserving one's own strength and punishing the enemy] ought to be sought. . . . In method it was fifty years ahead of the times."

But Lee's army also had suffered terribly, approximately thirty-two thousand casualties. This was a higher rate than Grant's in proportion to the size of Lee's total force, and an immensely higher rate in proportion to the manpower resources of the South. Lee was aware, too, that this kind of fighting would ultimately lock his army into a siege that could end only in defeat. Thus he continued to seek an opportunity to attack and achieve a decisive victory over the Army of the Potomac.

On June 13 Lee ordered General Jubal A. Early with thirteen

thousand troops to the Shenandoah Valley to clear this vital area of invaders and threaten Washington with a move north across the Potomac. Lee hoped to repeat the maneuver that had caused President Lincoln two years before to divert strength from McClellan's expedition. If Lincoln could be induced to make a similar diversion from Grant's army, perhaps Grant could be attacked successfully and destroyed, or at least forced to break off his offensive against Richmond.

On the day that Early left on his mission Lee learned that Grant was no longer before him. The Federal commander, convinced that the Confederates could not be broken by frontal attack and having no room left for a close flanking movement, was now marching to swing his army in a wide turning maneuver completely around Richmond on the east, cross the James River, and cut Lee's line of communication by seizing the Petersburg rail junction twenty miles south of the Confederate capital. The move was bold and brilliant both in conception and execution.

For once Lee failed to anticipate his opponent's intentions, a failure that allowed Grant to pass the James unmolested and throw his army in full strength upon his lightly held objective. Fortunately for Lee, Grant's attack at Petersburg was as poorly carried out as his march had been admirably executed, while the Confederate defense, conducted by General Beauregard against overwhelming numbers, was superb. When on June 17 Lee became convinced that the bulk of Grant's force was at Petersburg, Lee moved swiftly there, and the Union threat was, for the moment, ended.

The siege of Petersburg and Richmond now began, an ordeal that was to last for nine bitter months. Thus at midsummer of 1864 the major Union armies, Grant's in Virginia and Sherman's in Georgia, seemed hopelessly stalemated, the end of the war nowhere in sight. The morale of the northern population, already shaken by the appalling losses of the Virginia campaign, sank to a low ebb; the northern peace party grew alarmingly; and Lincoln began to believe that he could not be reelected in the 1864 presidential contest.

But Lee saw clearly the weakness of the Confederate military situation. His diversionary threat with Early's operation failed to accomplish its purpose though Early waged a remarkable campaign, driving the Federals from the Shenandoah Valley, crossing the Potomac, and actually making a weak assault on the outer defenses of Washington. Lee's instinct in launching this movement had been sound enough. Lincoln did become fearful for the safety of the capital and went so far as to suggest that Grant bring a part of his army back to protect the city.

Still the move failed to break Grant's iron grip on Petersburg. Instead, he eventually dispatched to the Valley a force under General Philip Sheridan that was sufficient to defeat Early while retaining at Petersburg a fortified siege line that was too powerful for Lee to assail with any prospect of success. Lee's only hope of escape was by abandoning Richmond altogether.

Lee discerned also that the Confederate defense of Georgia was in grave jeopardy. Sherman was now threatening Atlanta, and President Davis asked Lee's advice on a proposal to replace Sherman's opponent, the cautious General Joseph E. Johnston, with the younger and bolder Lieutenant General John Bell Hood. Averse to such a move, Lee said he yet hoped that Johnston would be able to save the city. As for Hood, who earlier had been an outstanding division commander in the Army of Northern Virginia, Lee this time was unusually explicit, saying that the subordinate general was indeed bold, but rash, and strongly implying that he was careless in his arrangements. Lee added the ominous and prescient warning that if Hood were placed in command, "We may lose Atlanta and the army."

Lee went further to suggest that if Atlanta could not be held, the Confederate army in Georgia ought to be withdrawn in the direction of Augusta near the eastern border of the state, and that all the Confederate cavalry west of the Appalachians be set upon Sherman's line of communication. This was perhaps as wise a strategy as any available to the Confederacy in its present situation. This strategy would have kept a strong Confederate force on Sherman's flank or rear and in position to make junction with Lee's army in an extremity. It would also have put Major General Nathan Bedford Forrest and his formidable Confederate cavalry to their most effective use. Sherman's greatest concern was the possibility that Forrest, whom he called a "very devil," might be employed in this manner.

Davis nevertheless replaced Johnston with Hood, who promptly launched a series of attacks against Sherman's larger army, was beaten, and on the last night in August withdrew from Atlanta. After the fall of this city and the final defeat of Early in the Shenandoah Valley (October 19), Lee saw the futility, from a strictly operational point of view, of attempting to defend Richmond any longer. He said the city had become a millstone about his neck. But he felt that only the president could make the momentous decision to abandon the capital. Lee also was keenly aware of the numbing effect that such a development would have on the morale of the southern population.

Instead, Lee continued to hold the Petersburg-Richmond line through the grim winter of 1864–65 while Sherman's army pillaged the lower South, as Lee had foreseen it would, destroying the transportation facilities, supplies, and popular morale required to support the operations of the Confederate armies.

At this critical moment in the war Lee openly endorsed the most revolutionary of all proposals for strengthening the southern war effort: the employment of black troops. With unanswerable logic he warned of the probability of Confederate defeat if such a step were not taken. Moreover, he said, the northern triumph would be attained partially through the use of southern blacks, who were being enrolled in substantial numbers in the Union army and would inevitably bring about emancipation.

He then urged the enrollment of slaves in the Confederate army, this action to be accompanied by the immediate emancipation of those who were enrolled, with emancipation to their families at the end of the war. He also expressed the opinion that the best means for getting the slaves to serve effectively as Confederate soldiers was the immediate adoption of a "well-digested" plan for general emancipation. He said after the war that he had advocated taking those steps on previous occasions. Nothing of consequence came of his recommendations.

Throughout the vicissitudes of the last year of the war, Lee remained the one symbol of southern invincibility. A movement now arose in the Confederate Congress to substitute him for Davis in the position of executive authority, and influential southern editors began to call for him to be made dictator in the manner of ancient Rome in war. Lee refused to listen to any such talk. Finally, in early February 1865 the Congress passed an act creating the position of general in chief, with Lee clearly in mind for the responsibility. Though Davis rightly considered this a vote of no confidence in his leadership, he swallowed his pride and signed the act; then he appointed Lee to the job.

A year earlier the naming of a general in chief by Davis could have yielded positive results, since it would have given a timely unity of command to the Confederate military effort and would have placed it in the hands of the one man who might have been capable of sustaining the confidence of the people, the legislators, the generals, and the troops. The time was now too late for any man or measure to save the flagging southern cause. Lee accepted the appointment, but in doing so he deliberately rebuked those who regarded the establishment of the position as a challenge to the president's authority as constitutional commander in chief of the armed forces. Lee said, "I am indebted alone to the kindness of his excellency, the president, for my nomination to this high and arduous office." He spoke as a reluctant generalissimo who saw the end in sight.

Lee nevertheless did everything possible within his legitimate authority to coordinate the remaining military resources of the South and keep the Confederacy alive. He persuaded Davis to restore General Joseph E. Johnston to command and sent Johnston to North Carolina with instructions to concentrate all of the scattered troops of the Confederacy there, except for Lee's own army, in an effort to stop Sherman.

Lee also conceived a plan to abandon Richmond when the spring weather had dried out the impassable roads of winter and when his starving horses had been strengthened by extra issues of his closely rationed corn. He intended to march south and join forces with Johnston for concerted blows, first against Sherman, then against Grant. Meanwhile, Lee exerted every effort to keep his famished, threadbare, and dispirited troops in fighting condition through the remainder of the winter. That under the prevailing circumstances he succeeded in doing so is a lasting tribute to his leadership.

On March 25 Lee made a diversionary attack on Fort Stedman near the center of the Union siege line in an effort to force Grant to withdraw troops from his extended left flank, which now blocked Lee's most direct route into North Carolina, the Weldon Railroad. The attempt was futile. Though the Confederates were able to seize the fort by a surprise assault and the ruse of dressing the attackers in Federal uniforms, Grant promptly retook the position and on April 2 countered by seizing another of Lee's lines of escape, the Southside Railroad at Five Forks. Richmond could no longer be held. During the night of April 2 Lee abandoned the long-defended trenches and marched west, intending to gain the Danville Railroad and make his way roundabout to a junction with Johnston.

The retreat was an ordeal of hunger, exhaustion, and despair. Lee reached the railroad at Amelia Court House only to lose a precious day in foraging because his order for rations had gone amiss. Before he could move his army south the Federals cut the railroad below him at Burkeville, forcing Lee to continue moving west, hoping somehow to outdistance his adversary and turn the corner to the south.

Grant pursued relentlessly. Sheridan's cavalry harassed the column at every step and on April 6 inflicted a sharp defeat on a portion of it at Sayler's Creek, where Lee lost some 7,700 men as prisoners and casualties. Only reverence for its commander held the destitute Confederate army together. A Confederate said later, "Lee was somewhere to the front, so his army followed." Many soldiers, however, did not follow. Great numbers, physically at the point of collapse and overcome with the futility of it all, dropped out of the ranks. Lee left Petersburg and Richmond with some thirty thousand men; after a week of marching and fighting, fewer than half that number remained in formation. The desperate trek was made in vain. Grant soon enveloped the faltering column, and on April 8 closed the route of escape near the village of Appomattox Court House.

Lee now knew for certain that the end had come for the Army of Northern Virginia, and for his own military career. Already he had received an invitation to surrender. A word from him, and the remaining troops doubtless would have sacrificed themselves in a suicidal assault upon the Union line. Lee chose surrender. When someone protested, "What will history say of the surrender of the army in the field?" Lee replied, "The question is, is it right to surrender this army? If it is right, then I will take all the responsibility."

One of Lee's most brilliant subordinates, Brigadier General E. Porter Alexander, suggested that he avoid capitulating by disbanding the army and permitting the men to scatter with their arms and report back to their state governments. In other words, they should resort to guerrilla warfare. Lee rejected the idea, saying: "General, you and I as Christian men have no right to consider how this would affect us. We must consider its effect on the country as a whole. . . . We would bring on a state of affairs it would take the country years to recover from. . . . The only dignified course for me would be to go to General Grant and surrender myself and take the consequences of my acts."

Thus Lee rode away at noon on April 9, 1865, to the dramatic meeting with Grant in the parlor of the McLean house in Appomattox Court House. There, with a simple but elemental dignity, he surrendered himself and the remnant of his army to his magnanimous adversary. When the terms of the transaction had been agreed upon, written down, and signed, Lee shook hands with Grant, bowed to the other officers present, and left the room. Outside the house he mounted his horse, Traveller, then rode slowly back to deliver the difficult news to his waiting army.

Lee's reception by his surrendered troops revealed perhaps more clearly than anything else in his career their devotion to him. A conqueror returning in triumph could not have expected a more stirring ovation than he received, except that Lee's ovation was rendered in sorrow rather than exultation. They cheered as he approached them. Addressing his soldiers from the saddle, he said, "Men, we have fought the war together, and I have done the best I could for you. You will all be paroled and go to your homes until exchanged." Then his eyes filled with tears and he could only add a broken, "Good-bye." He was immediately surrounded by a throng of sobbing, choking, shouting Confederates who looked up into his face, grasped at his hands, and poured out their affection for him unabashed. One grimy soldier reached up and shouted, "I love you just as well as ever, General Lee." Lee at last withdrew to be alone with his emotions.

The following day Lee issued his last formal order to his army: General Order No. 9, a farewell address. It praised the troops for their "unsurpassed courage and fortitude," and invoked upon them the blessing and protection of a merciful God. Lee concluded, "With an unceasing admiration of your constancy and devotion to your Country, and a grateful remembrance of your kind and generous consideration for myself, I bid you all an affectionate farewell."

By April 12 the Army of Northern Virginia was an army no more. Its muskets were stacked, its cannon parked, its battle flags furled, and its soldiers paroled to their destitute homes. That afternoon Lee left the field to return to his family in Richmond. Three days later he entered the charred and blasted city. He found the population awaiting his arrival, with a throng of spectators, including Federal soldiers, lining the streets to witness the passing procession.

It was a sight none of them ever forgot. They witnessed an escort of five war-worn officers, including Lee's son Rooney (Major General William Henry Fitzhugh Lee), mounted on jaded campaign horses and trailed by a half-dozen rickety and weathered ambulances and wagons, one of them covered with a patched quilt instead of canvas. Lee's presence transfigured the forlorn cavalcade. Erect astride his horse, with a countenance grave yet serene, he rode with measured gait through the expectant crowd. Cheers filled the air. Tears filled many eyes. Hats and service caps, including the great numbers of blue Union kepis among them, were lifted in respect as he passed. Lee bared his own head in response. When he reached the house on East Franklin Street where his wife and daughters lived, he dismounted, bowed to his admirers, entered, and closed the door. Then, in a simple but symbolically momentous act, he removed his sword forever.

After Appomattox

Evaluation

In the lapse of well over a century since Lee retired from the field his generalship has stood the test of time and circumstance. Even his severest critics, and there have been those, have admitted his talent as an army leader and field commander.

There is little cause to wonder that he emerged from the Civil War almost universally acclaimed by southerners as a leader without equal in either army of that conflict. In spite of his ultimate defeat, a great majority of Confederates at the war's end would have disagreed only slightly with the sentiment that he was invincible.

Southern biographers began at once to produce works of admiration and praise. Two years after the war John D. McCabe wrote of Lee as a "great soldier" and of the Army of Northern Virginia as the "great army which his [Lee's] genius made so glorious." Shortly afterward John Esten Cooke, a popular Virginia novelist, published a biography of Lee that he prefaced with the statement, "His military genius will always be conceded." The prominent Richmond journalist Edward A. Pollard, though not assigning Lee to the rank of genius, said he possessed "the almost perfect sum of qualities of a great military commander."

Writing a decade after the war the Reverend J. William Jones, once Lee's chaplain and now a chronicler of his life, expressed the South's collective estimate of him in saying, "We cannot doubt that the future historian, when he scans carefully all of the facts, will rank our noble chief the peer, if not the superior, of any soldier of either ancient or modern times." Beginning in the 1870s, the Southern Historical Society, under the guiding spirit of its president, the irascible ex-Confederate General Early, dedicated itself unremittingly to the exaltation of Lee's fame. The popular Virginia novelist and historian Thomas Nelson Page, writing in the early years of the twentieth century, affirmed that history might be searched in vain for Lee's superior, and that only once or twice could his equal be found.

Most southerners of the twentieth century have only somewhat qualified the earlier appraisals of Lee. In 1942 Lee's celebrated biographer, Freeman, expressed a great southern consensus in summing up his estimate of Lee's generalship: "When the remorseless audit of history discounts the odds he faced in men and resources, and when the court of time writes up the advantage he enjoyed in fighting on inner lines in his own country, the balance to the credit of his generalship is clear and absolute."

Nor have southerners been alone in their high evaluation of Lee's military prowess. Many northern students of the war have shared this view. Historian James Ford Rhodes, writing in the 1890s, affirmed that Lee's leadership was the primary source of the remarkable Confederate resistance. John C. Ropes and W. R. Livermore, in a multivolume work on the war published in the early twentieth century, said of Lee, "No [other] army commander on either side was so universally believed in, so absolutely trusted. Nor was there ever a commander who better deserved the support of his Government and the affection and confidence of his soldiers."

Many of the tributes to Lee's generalship came from abroad. A perceptive English officer who visited the United States and met Lee—General Viscount Garnet J. Wolseley—judged him to be the greatest of all American generals. Colonel G. F. R. Henderson, who is ranked among the keenest of the contemporary British military analysts, went even further in his praise of Lee by calling him "one of the greatest, if not the greatest soldier, who ever spoke the English tongue."

Sir Frederick Maurice, a twentieth-century British student of both ancient and modern military affairs, wrote with World War I in his perspective to place Lee among the top martial leaders of all history. Cyril Falls, an eminent British military historian of the post–World War II era, said in a study of the world's greatest commanders of modern times, "Lee alone in a century of warfare deserves to be ranked with Hannibal and Napoleon."

Lee's military reputation nevertheless attracted a drumfire of criticism down through the years. Much of this criticism was either hastily conceived or ill informed. Often the indictments of his leadership contradicted one another. He was accused of dangerous rashness and impulsiveness, but also of excessive caution and indecision. He was found guilty of failing to take strategic advantage of the South's inner lines of communication, but he was also charged with a preoccupation with the outworn concept of the employment of inner lines. He was arraigned for a failure to appreciate the principle of the concentration of force, or again for placing too much faith in the importance of concentration. Lee obviously cannot be held accountable on all of these conflicting points.

A more serious impeachment of Lee's generalship occurred in 1933 with the publication of a study by a prominent British officer and military historian, General J. F. C. Fuller, who compared Lee unfavorably with his chief antagonist, Grant. Fuller accused Lee of a weakness in logistical ability that resulted in a failure to supply his army adequately, but the British critic offered no convincing explanation of what Lee as an army commander could have done to remedy the inadequacy of the southern commissary and transportation systems, which were the major causes of the shortages.

Fuller also argued that although Lee possessed a remarkable capacity to inspire his troops, he was unable to direct his army so as to carry out his designs: he failed to "stamp his mind" upon his operations. This is indeed a curious accusation. Lee's operations were the direct product of his mind, and it is difficult to conceive how they did not bear the stamp of it. Moreover, he decidedly placed the stamp of his mind upon his opponents' operations, so much so that the celebrated Civil War author Bruce Catton would write, "Among the many achievements of this remarkable man, nothing is more striking than his ability to dominate the minds of the men who were fighting against him."

In addition to disparaging Lee as an army commander, Fuller believed his strategic thinking was faulty. The Briton argued that the Confederacy ought to have concentrated its forces in the vicinity of Chattanooga, temporarily yielding Virginia and other regions to the Federals. In this manner, he said, the Confederates could have harassed their enemies' lengthening lines of communication and ultimately might have defeated them decisively once they were drawn deep into the South.

In pure theory, as a sand-table exercise in strategy, Fuller's plan may have been sound, though many objections come to mind. As a practical strategy for the Confederacy it would have been disastrous. It would have required surrendering indefinitely to the enemy the entire upper South and the Atlantic coastal states, a proposition that would have been outrageous to President Davis and to the southern population in general. An equivalent strategy today would call for the surrender of everything in the United States above the Potomac, Ohio, and Missouri Rivers and west of the Rocky Mountains. Fuller's plan ignored the political, economic, social, and psychological realities of southern life. Lee, on the other hand, insightfully adapted his strategy to those very factors.

Other indictments of Lee's generalship began in the period after World War II, an event that prompted certain students of military affairs to measure his strategy and performance against the modern concepts of "total" and "global" war. A number of critics have come to believe that, according to this gauge, he falls short of the foremost Union military leaders. They say that although Lee was a brilliant practitioner of conventional warfare in the limited theater of Virginia, he was too provincial to see the Civil War as a whole, and too conservative to adopt new methods of combat. In this view, Grant and Sherman emerge as prototypes of modern military thinkers; Lee as an outstanding old-fashioned general.

These are telling criticisms and deserve careful examination. Did Lee permit an inordinate concern for the defense of Virginia to prevent him from conceiving or endorsing a comprehensive strategy that might have achieved victory for the South or, at least, have come closer to achieving it? Many of his modern critics believe that the plan of western concentration advanced in the spring of 1863 by Beauregard, Joseph E. Johnston, Longstreet, and others, and rejected by Lee, the plan for transporting a significant portion of his army to the West, might have been such a strategy. These critics emphasize that the Confederacy actually lost the war in the West, and that a timely shift of troops might have given the massed southern forces there the strength to destroy the Union armies piecemeal.

No one, of course, can ever really know what the outcome of such a move would have been. The proposition is theoretical, the result speculative. Possibly the strategy could have succeeded. But its success would have depended on a number of circumstances that cannot be taken for granted, and which the Confederacy was unable to compel.

The Union army in Virginia, the most powerful of all, would have been obliged to stand idle all the while, else Virginia and the East might have fallen, and the war have been lost in the East. The Union army in Tennessee would have had to remain inert and exposed to destruction while the Confederacy massed her strength against it. The southern railroads, already taxed beyond capacity, would have been required to deliver the various far-flung contingents to the point of concentration with a speed and precision never attained in practice. The hastily assembled Confederate striking force would then have found it necessary to operate unhampered by the very miscarriages that befell the efficient Army of Northern Virginia in the Gettysburg campaign and the reinforced Army of Tennessee in the Chickamauga-Chattanooga campaign.

That the proposed plan for western concentration would have enjoyed any of these advantages is questionable. That it would have enjoyed all of them is impossible to imagine. As already seen, when the plan was attempted later, it ended in failure. The grand strategy that Lee is taken to task for rejecting is itself open to serious criticism. Viewed from the perspective of the spring of 1863, following Chancellorsville, Lee was right in believing that the Army of Northern Virginia, commanded by him, was much likelier to win a decisive victory in the East than was a thrown-together force under someone else somewhere in the West.

Then should Lee not have acceded to a suggestion by Davis that Lee accompany a portion of his army to the West and command the enlarged Confederate force there? This sounds like a promising idea. But such a move would have changed none of the conditions discussed above. It would have represented only a change in commanders. Also, it would have created other serious, possibly fatal, disadvantages for the Confederates. Lee's transfer from Virginia to Tennessee would have "telegraphed" the Confederate intentions as clearly as if the Union authorities had been sent a copy of the plan. For them to fail to respond by reinforcing Rosecrans or launching a powerful attack in Virginia, or both simultaneously, is unthinkable. Moreover, such a plan would have forfeited altogether the most important strategic advantage of the Army of Northern Virginia: its threat to Washington and the East.

Was Lee indeed blind to the war as a whole, incapable of conceiving a strategy for the entire Confederacy? To consider this question fairly, one must keep in mind that until virtually the end of the war he was the commander of a single army, and that his own mission was limited to the defense of Richmond and northern Virginia. He can hardly be censured for failing to produce a fully developed war plan under these circumstances. But an examination of his various proposals made in the fall of 1862 and spring of 1863 reveals that Lee did in fact offer, at least in outline, a coherent strategy for the South.

Lee aimed his strategy at what Clausewitz would have called the Union's "center of gravity," which Lee unerringly identified as the northern faith in victory and will to continue the war. His strategy for destroying this faith and will involved strengthening his own army with reinforcements from relatively idle points along the lower Atlantic and Gulf coasts, and employing it as the major striking force of the Confederacy. Concerted southern offensives in the western theater would be mounted to protect the region until the main Confederate effort by his army could take effect. All of these operations were to be accompanied by a peace overture by the Confederate government designed to promote the growth of a formidable peace movement in the North. This combination of military and diplomatic strategies was the nearest thing the Confederacy ever had to a comprehensive national strategy for winning the war. It probably was as likely to do so as any other plan open to the South.

Was Lee too conservative, his mind too fixed, to break with tradition and employ new military methods? Some recent students of the war believe he was so dedicated to offensive action that he failed to take advantage of the economy in lives provided by the defensive, the strength of which had been enhanced by the recently perfected rifled musket, a weapon of increased range and accuracy. In other words, he employed eighteenth-century tactics against nineteenth-century armaments. Certainly, Lee on occasion ordered attacks that failed and were prohibitively costly in casualties. Malvern Hill and Gettysburg were the chief instances of this. But a policy committed, a priori, to the tactical defensive by Lee would have been a recipe for certain defeat. It would have surrendered the initiative to the enemy, permitting him to concentrate his vastly superior numbers against Lee and to select the place and time of battle.

Or, Lee's opponent would have been able to turn Lee's defensive positions if he chose to do so, as Burnside attempted to do at Fredericksburg, Hooker did at Chancellorsville only to be beaten by Lee's counterattack, and Grant did in passing the James River and, after bungling in the attack on Petersburg, establishing the siege that immobilized Lee and eventually defeated him. Wisely, Lee made his decisions to defend or attack in response to the ever-shifting strategic, operational, and tactical circumstances of the moment.

Ideally, of course, he should have fought only under conditions that would have enabled him to win such low-cost victories as Fredericksburg or Cold Harbor. But he knew that it was not always possible. In spite of costly mistakes on rare occasions, his record supports Clausewitz's dictum, "Happy the army in which an untimely boldness frequently manifests itself." This "untimely boldness," the willingness to take the calculated risk, was a vital quality in Lee's effectiveness as a general.

Even Lee's attacks at Malvern Hill and Gettysburg were not inevitably doomed to fail. They failed because of errors made by him or his subordinates in the execution of the attacks, and by the astute dispositions of his opponents in taking advantage of these errors. In other words, they failed because of superior Union tactical leadership at the particular place and time, and because of the ever-present elements of what Clausewitz called *friction:* those involving decision, calculation, risk, misunderstanding, and chance and uncertainty on the battlefield.

It is true that in his attacks Lee suffered more casualties on average than in his defensive actions. But, significantly, in the aggregate of casualties incurred in the battles in which he launched attacks (Seven Days, Second Manassas, Chancellorsville, Gettysburg, and the Wilderness), he demonstrated that in addition to the strategic advantages to be gained from successful attacks (the aborting of Federal offensives) he was able through superior leadership to inflict on the enemy more casualties by almost eight thousand than his own army suffered.

In a number of his attacks, the casualty ratios were as favorable to him, or more so, as those of a number of his defensive battles. For example, at Second Manassas and again at Chancellorsville (attacks by Lee), he inflicted more casualties both in absolute numbers and in proportion to those he suffered than at Antietam (a defensive battle by Lee). The casualty figures on both sides in the Wilderness (an attack by Lee) were almost identical to those at Spotsylvania (a defensive battle by Lee). Lee's willingness to attack ought to be judged against its overall effects throughout the war, not merely against the number of casualties suffered in particular battles.

His decisions to invade the North have been the subject of especially sharp criticism. But his failures in the invasions were tactical, not strategic, in that he failed to win a decisive victory in the field in either endeavor. Neither of these operations failed as the result of the offensive strategy. Possibly the failure of the Maryland invasion in the fall of 1862 was caused by the chance discovery of Lee's march orders. Certainly, the outcome was heavily influenced by this episode.

His boldness in seizing the strategic initiative in the Gettysburg campaign, coupled with his operational skill in executing the movement, gained him a precious numerical tactical advantage. In all of his Virginia battles, whether he attacked or defended, he faced numerical odds approaching one to two. But despite his lack of information on the enemy at Gettysburg, he engaged in battle there at numerical odds of only about seven to nine, and on the first day of the encounter he actually enjoyed a numerical superiority on the field, for the only time in the war.

The Confederacy had much to gain from a victory in either of his northern invasions. A victory such as Second Manassas or Chancellorsville in either of these campaigns probably would not have fulfilled Lee's hope of ending the war, but it certainly would have dealt a severe blow to the already-flagging northern morale. A decisive victory in the Maryland campaign in 1862 probably would have resulted in some form of European intervention in the war; it also would have prevented the Emancipation Proclamation at that time.

In spite of Lee's failure to achieve the larger goal of his invasions of the North, those campaigns did accomplish one important end. They protected his right flank and rear against the constant threat of being turned through Union naval control of the Chesapeake and the Atlantic seaboard. McClellan attempted to exploit this Union advantage but was defeated, in part by Lee's strategy of having Jackson make an offensive move in the Shenandoah Valley, thus causing Lincoln to withhold McDowell's corps from McClellan.

A more serious threat of a Union turning maneuver from the sea came from Grant. When in January 1864 President Lincoln was preparing to elevate Grant to the position of general in chief, the president had General Henry Halleck write and ask for his proposals for winning the war. Among other suggestions, Grant indicated that he would land a force of sixty thousand on the coast below Richmond and move against Lee's supply lines. Grant believed this operation would force Lee to abandon northern Virginia, and Lee himself admitted he would be obliged to do so if such a Union move should be successful.

Whether Grant's proposed strategy would have worked cannot be known, but Halleck's reply made explicit the strategic importance of Lee's threats against Washington in protecting his flank and rear. Halleck vetoed Grant's plan, saying it would require dividing the Army of the Potomac, with Lee between the two wings, thus exposing the capital to an unacceptable risk. As a result, Grant was compelled during the spring and summer of 1864 to fight his grueling campaign directly against Lee's army, a campaign so bloody that Union morale again withered alarmingly.

Another school of Lee's critics believe he should have avoided pitched battles altogether. The Confederacy should have adopted the traditional strategy of the weaker side, they argue: yielding territory and resorting to wholesale guerrilla warfare. By so doing, they believe, the South ultimately could have exhausted the northern will to carry on the war. Historical examples of the success of such a policy are cited to support this contention.

As already discussed, the idea of continuing the war by guerrilla action was suggested by General E. Porter Alexander and rejected by Lee just before Appomattox. Shortly after Lee's surrender, Jefferson Davis began to consider a form of guerrilla warfare.

That in the beginning of the war the southern people would have supported a policy of giving up the land without fighting pitched battles to protect it is extremely doubtful. Certainly, Davis would not have tolerated a general who proposed to do so at that time. The evidence powerfully suggests that at the end of the war the majority of the southern people, traumatized by four years of furious combat and enormous bloodshed and destruction, would not have approved a continuation of the struggle by any means.

Beyond a doubt, with Lee's blessing, the South could have

waged a formidable guerrilla war. The other Confederate generals
would have followed his example in disbanding their armies, thus
setting loose such "devils" as Forrest on the scene. In all probability, this ultimately would have failed to achieve Confederate
independence. Meanwhile, it would have visited indescribable
physical, political, economic, and social havoc upon a South
that already lay crushed by the war of armies. It would have inflamed sectional hostilities to a point that a true national reunion,
a spiritual reunion, would have been virtually impossible; it would
have ignited unquenchable class and racial hatreds within the
region. For Lee's decision to surrender with dignity and finality,
all Americans owe him an incalculable debt of gratitude.

Was Lee too old-fashioned to break with tradition and use
new military methods? In some ways he assuredly seemed conventional and even old-fashioned. His orders against looting and
molesting private property while on the march in Pennsylvania
sound positively quaint beside Grant's instructions that the
Shenandoah Valley be stripped so bare that a crow flying over it
would be obliged to carry its own rations, or beside Sherman's
description of his plans for devastating the roads, houses, and
people of Georgia.

Some have concluded from the contrast between Lee's orders
and the statements of the Union commanders that Lee failed to
see the connection between the disruption of a nation's civilian
economy and the destruction of its military capacity, or that Lee's
genteel code of conduct rendered him incapable of accepting
the realities of modern warfare. This is an arresting thought: that
the foremost scion of a land defending slavery and secession
should turn out to be too humane to employ the ruthless methods
of warfare being used against him by the supporters of freedom
and union.

Unquestionably, Lee's sense of gentility was outraged by acts
of wanton cruelty to civilians. Yet his warning in the winter of 1864

of the effects of Sherman's forthcoming march through the lower South indicated clear insight into the military consequences of the loss of Georgia's factories, provisions, and railroads. Concerning his own methods, Lee had sound reasons for seeking to prevent his troops from indulging in an orgy of plundering while in Pennsylvania. He appreciated the absolute necessity for speed, march cohesion, and discipline in the presence of a powerful enemy army, and he knew that pillaging would render such discipline impossible.

Moreover, he believed that the behavior of his troops would influence the attitude of the northern population, encouraging the peace party there, and of the European governments. He also believed this behavior would influence the attitude of God. On the effect of troop conduct, a distinguished British military analyst and historian, Captain B. H. Liddell Hart, has written, "Chivalry in war can be a most effective weapon in weakening the opponent's will to resist, as well as augmenting [one's own army's] moral strength." Perhaps Lee discerned between his measures and his objectives a connection his critics have failed to detect.

Lee has been accused of slack discipline. Measured by the standards of professional armies he was indeed guilty. Sir Frederick Maurice admitted as much about him but explained that a Prussian mode of discipline would have destroyed his army of individualistic southerners.

Lee corroborated Maurice's statement in explaining why he refused to remove Brigadier General Ambrose R. Wright of Georgia from command after Wright allegedly had failed to perform satisfactorily on one occasion. "These men are not an army," Lee said. "They are citizens defending their country. General Wright is not a soldier; he is a lawyer. I cannot do many things that I could do with a trained [professional] army."

Lee went on to say that the people of Georgia would be

offended by an action that would humiliate General Wright, and that there was no one better qualified to fill Wright's place. Then Lee came to the essence of his method of discipline in dealing with the citizen soldiers of the Confederacy. "When a man makes a mistake I call him to my tent and use the authority of my position to make him do the right thing next time." Lee's method achieved to an unsurpassed degree the true object of military discipline: to establish cohesion in bodies of men and instill in the individual soldiers a willingness to carry out their duty under extreme stress and hazard.

Some have faulted Lee for issuing discretionary orders instead of peremptory commands. This has been identified as a weakness of character, or as the product of an excessive amiability. Assuredly, there were occasions when Lee's method failed to bring about the desired result. But only by the use of such orders can a commanding general ensure the flexibility required to cope with Clausewitz's chance and uncertainty in battle. One of the most distinguished American generals of the twentieth century, General Matthew Ridgway, concluded that the use of discretionary orders would be an imperative for success in wars of the future. If this mode of command caused Lee to suffer some defeats, it gained him even more victories.

Lee is said to have failed to appreciate the role of a modern staff, and to have kept his own staff too low in rank to be of any vital service. True, Lee's staff was light in comparison with Grant's; the highest rank in Lee's staff was that of colonel, while Grant's staff included ranks as exalted as that of major general. A stronger staff would have alleviated Lee's burden of communications, but that it would have enhanced the effectiveness of his generalship cannot be demonstrated.

If, as some have argued, a weakness of staff was to blame for mistakes by Lee in the Gettysburg campaign, this same weakness ought to be credited with his successes on various other occasions. One can scarcely imagine a Second Manassas or Chancellorsville, for example, being conceived and executed through the collaboration of a set of high-ranking staff officers. These victories were the product of direct, on-the-ground decisions, orders, and instructions by Lee. Moreover, Grant's heavy staff seems to have been useless to him in the operation where it ought to have been the most useful, the approach and initial attack on Petersburg. Possibly, the relative smallness of Lee's army is what made his command methods work so well so often. He ought not be faulted for failing to invent something that he did not need.

Many decisions and actions by Lee refute the accusation that he was too committed to the past to be able to adopt methods of warfare suited to his own time or to the future. He violated countless sacrosanct strategic and tactical rules, he pioneered the strategic use of railroads, he was preeminent in the science of field fortification, he instantly endorsed a proposal for massing his field artillery so as to provide maximum support at the most critical points of the battle, and he improvised the weapon of railway artillery in order to give mobility to the heavy guns guarding the river approaches to Richmond. Such actions indicate a readiness to part with outmoded ways in the field.

Even more impressive were Lee's ideas concerning the very nature of war. His early prediction of the length and severity of the Civil War; his foresight in urging conscription and total mobilization of southern resources; his often-successful efforts to play upon President Lincoln's and General Halleck's fears for the safety of Washington; his resort to psychological warfare by appealing to the northern peace party and seeking to split the mind of the enemy; his canny use of all kinds of information sources, especially northern newspapers; his modification of theoretical military principles to fit the demands of the southern political, economic, and social realities; and his support of the employment of black troops to be followed by emancipation all indicate a concept of military affairs that went far beyond the battlefield. These judgments and measures were hardly the products of a tradition-bound mind.

Lee's greatest shortcoming for the role in which fate had cast him was not a fault in generalship. It was his lack of an implacable revolutionary purpose. In a situation comparable to Lee's, a Napoleon doubtless would have seized the reins of authority; would have appealed to the spirit of the southern population with the inspiration of his own name; would have commandeered the railroads, equipment, and provisions needed by his armies; would have enrolled the blacks in his depleted ranks, with emancipation as the reward for faithful service; would have concentrated the scattered troops of the South for decisive blows at the enemy.

Lee was aware of the imperatives of the hour; he was also aware that the people's support was his for the taking. But he would hear no talk of a coup d'état against the civil administration. Thus, by an ironic turn of circumstance, Lee's ultimate weakness as a Confederate leader was the product of one of his most admirable qualities. He was too American to play Napoleon.

Instead, he remained deferential, possibly excessively so, to Davis as the constitutional commander in chief of the Confederate armed forces. Even in accepting his last-hour appointment as general in chief, Lee expressed his gratitude to Davis. Lee has been criticized for this deference. One should bear in mind, however, that in this way he was able to assure Davis's support of him and his army in return. This mutual respect and friendship between Lee and Davis was an essential element in Lee's success in the field and in the maintenance of Confederate resistance. Generals who crossed Davis, such as Joseph E. Johnston and Beauregard, soon lost their roles as major figures in the prosecution of the war.

Lee's deep feeling of responsibility as a military commander, coupled with his sense of subordination to the constitutional commander in chief, has subjected Lee to the harshest of the criticisms launched against him: that the blood shed during the last several months of the war, allegedly after the hope of Confederate victory had vanished, is on his hands, and that in continuing to fight he compromised his honor as a soldier. Objective students of the ethics of command will exonerate him of this charge. He was obligated to fight as long as the civil authorities chose to do so, and as long as his army had the capacity to do so. It possessed this capacity until just before the end.

Lee's prowess sprang from the major qualities of his being: intellect, audacity, poise, bearing, and character. Endowed with a superior intellect, he had cultivated it with care and prepared it diligently for the work it was to do. The "accurate reasoning of a trained and precise mind," says Freeman perceptively, provided Lee with an outstanding aptitude for the "difficult synthesis of war." Intellect made it possible for Lee to read his opponents' intentions, doubts, and fears with such accuracy that he appeared at times to be clairvoyant.

Lee once explained his ability to anticipate enemy moves by saying he simply assumed his opponent would do what he (Lee) would do in the same circumstances. Actually, Lee often did what his opponent would not have done. Again, it was intellect that enabled Lee to take advantage of his insights with extraordinary resourcefulness.

Audacity prompted Lee to follow the course of action suggested by intellect. He possessed that boldness that Clausewitz likened to "the true steel which gives the weapon its edge and brilliancy." Boldness moved Lee time and again to seize the initiative from adversaries of almost twice his strength, and to abandon hallowed operational doctrines in order to deliver his blows at the least expected times and places. He himself best expressed the importance of this capacity when he said on the eve of a daring operation, "We must decide between the positive loss of inactivity and the risk of action." Lee's willingness to take the risk of action lay at the core of his generalship.

Lee's poise, his clarity of mind in the sound and fury of battle, his ability to think and act under fire and stress, and his capacity to respond effectively to the chance and uncertainty of combat were qualities in which he excelled. Most of the time he did not permit his emotions to influence his operational or tactical decisions, but maintained his poise even in his attitude toward the enemy, whom he customarily referred to as "those people," though on occasions of hot anger, or perhaps in an effort to stir his troops to superhuman exertion, he condemned the Union soldiers as vandals. Probably Chancellorsville offered the supreme military demonstration of his intellectual acuteness and ingenuity, poise, and audacity, but all of his battles, with the exception of Gettysburg, gave comparable examples.

Beyond doubt, Lee's appearance and bearing—his presence—enhanced his attributes of mind and personality to enable him to exert a profound influence on his soldiers and all others who came in contact with him. Having sat in a single conference with Lee, General Viscount Wolseley wrote, "I have met many of the great men of my time, but Lee alone impressed me with the feeling that I was in the presence of a man who was cast in a grander mould, and made of different and finer metal than all other men. He is stamped upon my memory as a being apart and superior to all others in every way: a man with whom none I ever knew, a very few of whom I have ever read, are worthy to be classed."

An Irish traveler and observer who met Lee near the end of the war described him in language fully as strong as Wolseley's. He called Lee the idol of his soldiers and the hope of his people; said he was the handsomest man in all that constitutes dignity that he [the observer] had ever seen; and was one of the most prepossessing figures who had ever borne the weight of command or led the fortunes of a nation. Finally, said the Irish traveler, the southern people held an almost fanatical belief in Lee's judgment and sagacity.

Union Brigadier General Joshua Chamberlain, who witnessed Lee as he rode to meet Grant at Appomattox Court House, never forgot the experience. Chamberlain said that as Lee approached, he felt a "mysterious and powerful presence" come over the scene.

A vivid demonstration of the electric effect of Lee's presence on his troops occurred when Longstreet's divisions returned from Tennessee to the Army of Northern Virginia. Lee welcomed them with a review. When he rode onto the field and bared his head, the tatterdemalion soldiers shouted and wept and waved their battle flags. Passing slowly down the line, he looked into every face; all felt the powerful bond that held them together. To Brigadier General E. Porter Alexander, the effect was that of a "military sacrament."

Yet all of these qualities would not of themselves have produced such a leader as Lee. His greatest source of strength was that elusive and indefinable quality called character, the quality that provides the moral flame of leadership. Doubtless this trait in him grew out of a mingling of his profound religious conviction with the sense of honor and propriety of the Virginia gentry.

Whatever its origins, character was the foundation of Lee's generalship. Including Lee along with Alexander the Great, Hannibal, Julius Caesar, and Napoleon, a distinguished, mid-twentieth-century British student of military leadership, F. E. Adcock, wrote, "[They] had the highest faculties of mind. . . . But they possessed character in a still greater degree." A German scholar on war, Major General Hugo von Freytag-Loringhoven, included Lee in his list of the great military leaders of modern history, and said of them: "[They] acquired the ability to inspire great effort and self-sacrifice in others by strict self-discipline and strong religious faith. The purity of their characters was so evident that they seemed to be the incarnation of the ideal leader formulated by Clausewitz."

The combination of Lee's qualities inspired an almost-unmatched confidence among his soldiers, a confidence that enabled them frequently to accomplish what appeared to be impossible. A captain in Longstreet's corps, writing from Tennessee to his wife after having fought both at Gettysburg and Chickamauga, best expressed this feeling when he wrote: "The difference between this army [Bragg's] and Lee's is very striking. When the men move in the Army of Northern Virginia, they think it is the proper thing, whether it be backward or forward, and if all the success anticipated is not secured, at all events, it is not Lee's fault." No general could wish for a greater tribute.

Paradoxically, the most eloquent testimony to Lee's leadership came from one of his severest critics, General Fuller. Despite his reservations about Lee's command judgments and technical abilities, when Fuller stood back and surveyed the effects of Lee's leadership he was moved to say, "Few generals have been able to animate an army as Lee's self-sacrificing idealism animated the Army of Northern Virginia." And again, "What this bootless, ragged, half-starved army accomplished is one of the miracles of history."

Notwithstanding Lee's mistakes and weaknesses, whether real or imagined, his generalship was the crux of the Confederacy's extraordinary military effort. Massively outnumbered in the field and operating under virtually every other handicap known to war, he repeatedly brought the Union to the edge of despair. That anyone else could have done more is beyond demonstration. It challenges credibility.

At Peace

If Lee the soldier was venerated by the people of the South and respected by a host of people in the North, Lee the man of peace became in the eyes of many throughout the nation a symbol of the noblest qualities of both southern and American life. Amid the chaos and despair of his defeated state and region he stood firm and serene, refusing to indulge in self-pity or to join groups of his former associates in voluntary exile to Brazil, Mexico, or elsewhere. "Now, more than at any other time," he said to an acquaintance, "Virginia and every other state in the South needs us. We must try and, with as little delay as possible, go to work to build up their prosperity." To another he wrote, "I cannot desert my native state in the hour of her adversity. I must abide her fortunes, and share her fate."

Advising fellow southerners to lay aside old animosities and rear their children to be Americans, Lee became a potent force in the efforts to erase the sectional animosities that had caused the Civil War and had been immensely inflamed by it. From the day when he rode back from the surrender at Appomattox Court House until the moment he lay on his deathbed more than five years afterward, he devoted himself unswervingly to the task of rebuilding the South and restoring her to a position of honor, dignity, and usefulness within the reunited nation.

Aware that countless ex-Confederates looked to him for guidance in their behavior toward the victorious United States government, he chose his course carefully and gave advice sparingly. But he did offer measured counsel: work hard, he told his fellow citizens, keep silent on controversial issues, and avoid any action that might draw the wrath or vengeance of the North. When he heard harsh things said about Federal officials, he replied by pointing out instances of their generosity. Of his great antagonist in the field, he said, "General Grant has acted with magnanimity." When asked what he would do if Grant should visit his town, Lee replied that he would invite him into his home and act toward him as one gentleman to another. In other words, Lee offered to the proud and impulsive but defeated and angry South the priceless admonition of diligence, discretion, self-discipline, and courtesy.

When he learned that he was among the classes unaffected by the general terms of President Andrew Johnson's amnesty proclamation of May 29, 1865, and that a move was afoot to indict and try him for treason, he decided to take advantage of the provision that permitted excluded individuals to apply for pardon. Urged by General Meade to take this step as an important symbolic move in the restoration of amicable relations between the South and the rest of the nation, Lee on July 13 filed his application. As events turned out, he was never brought to trial, but, though General Grant solicited pardon for him, he did not receive it.

For more than a century the belief prevailed that Lee was not pardoned because he had failed to include with his application a required oath of allegiance to the United States. But eventually his signed oath was discovered in the holdings of the National Archives. Because he was initially unaware that an oath was required, Lee submitted it after filing the application for pardon, and the oath never reached the President's desk. In 1975, as a result of the discovery of the oath, the United States government restored Lee's full rights of citizenship.

Lee reinforced his advice that southerners go to work by promptly doing so himself. He refused lucrative offers of positions from former Confederates who had fought under his command and who prospered after the war. He rejected a profitable sinecure with a New York firm engaged in business in the South with the simple but crushing rebuke that he could not accept money for the use of his name without his time and labor. He also turned down an overture by a wealthy English admirer who wished to establish him on one of the man's estates.

Lee even gave up his own dream of settling on a small farm, "some little, quiet place in the woods," suppressing the yearning of a weary man in his sixties for a few years of rest in the twilight of life. Instead, when in August 1865 he received an invitation to become the president of a small, bankrupt college in Lexington, Virginia—Washington College—he accepted without delay. Thus he chose the course of simplicity and service over that of affluence and ease.

He took up his new duties in the fall of the same year. Revealing his vision of the role of education in revitalizing the South, he said: "I consider the proper education of youth one of the most important objects now to be attained, and one from which the greatest benefits may be expected. Nothing will compensate us for the depression of the standard of our moral and intellectual culture, and each state should take the most energetic measures to revive its schools and colleges, and, if possible, to increase the facilities of instruction and to elevate the standard of living."

He was, of course, urgently aware that his role of command in the Civil War placed him in an unusual, if not unique, relationship to the youth of the South. "I have a self-imposed task which I must accomplish," he said. "I have seen many of them fall under my standard. I shall devote all my life now to training young men to do their duty in life."

He set about at once to restore and expand the war-stricken institution. Gradually he broadened the curriculum, added schools of engineering and law, and erected new buildings. The enrollment increased steadily with the advancing years. Students came from throughout the South, men who bore the memories and often the scars of battle, as well as boys away from home for the first time, all attracted by Lee's presence. He introduced both the elective system of courses and the honor system of discipline.

Lee's zeal for education burgeoned as he directed the affairs of the college. He emphasized the importance of the classics and of cultural studies generally, and he looked upon informal moral and religious training as the highest goal of the school, saying on one occasion, "If I could only know that all the young men in the college were good Christians, I should have nothing more to desire." His greatest personal contribution to the training of his students was in the development of character, honor, and dignity. He was acquainted with every student individually and thus was able to communicate directly a measure of his own qualities.

He told newcomers that the school had no printed rules. "We have but one rule here," he said, "and it is that every student must be a gentleman." Infractions and derelictions did, of course, occur under this lofty policy, but Lee's own dignity and self-mastery, combined with the awe inspired by his fame, reduced the problems of keeping order.

His conviction that the training of the South's youth was essential to the future material development of the region power-fully influenced his mind in shaping the curriculum of the college. Just as he had refused to be bound by tradition in his military thinking, he now would not be fettered by conventional ideas on education. Recognizing the need for practical and professional training, he promoted courses in agriculture, commerce, applied chemistry, history, modern languages, and journalism, along with an expansion of the program in engineering to include civil, mechanical, and mining engineering. He was said to have had in mind the establishment of a medical school if sufficient funds could be obtained for it. Within the limits of the college's financial and physical resources, he made it into a model of advanced educational practices. Freeman wrote, "Defeated in war, Lee triumphed in his labor to upbuild the South."

Lee continued to exercise immense influence over the attitude of the southern people toward the rest of the nation. But his role as oracle, counselor, and exemplar became more difficult as the Federal government applied coercive measures of Reconstruction to the defeated region.

In February 1866 he was called to appear before the Congressional Joint Committee on Reconstruction, a group dominated by Radical Republicans who advocated stern treatment for the former Confederate states. Calmly, he expressed his convictions that southerners were not contemplating a renewal of the rebellion against the Federal authorities, that neither he nor others had committed treason in fighting for the Confederacy, that the war itself could have been avoided by wisdom and forbearance on both sides, and that liberality on the part of the victorious North would help to heal the nation's wounds.

The portion of his testimony that most offends modern critics has to do with the sensitive and controversial question of the status of the former slaves in Virginia. Under direct interrogation he said he felt that the state would be better off if it could be rid of them, and that he had long held this belief. He said also that to permit them to vote immediately would be a mistake because they were not qualified for the franchise and would be easily led by demagogues.

Today, of course, these ideas are anathema. But Lee's statements need to be judged in the light of his own day. Questions about the place of blacks in the American society were then extremely unsettled in the American mind. In formulating an emancipation policy, Lincoln had believed that both blacks and whites would be benefitted by an exodus of the blacks. He had urged them to leave this country and encouraged efforts to colonize them elsewhere. He had suggested only a token black franchise in Louisiana for the purpose of inducing the Congress to accept the state back into the Union; he had never advocated black suffrage for the states of the North.

Even as Lee spoke to the congressional committee, many northern states, despite having only a relatively negligible number of blacks in their populations, continued to deny them the rights of voting and holding public office. Recent elections in the North indicated a rising opposition to black suffrage there. A few weeks earlier the voters of Connecticut had rejected a measure to extend the ballot to the state's two thousand blacks. A month later the voters of Michigan and Wisconsin took similar steps.

Lee anticipated the actions of Congress that ultimately occurred: the passage of a series of measures that in effect placed the former Confederate states under Federal military authority, which soon created state governments in which blacks voted and held office. His apprehension over this expansion of Federal authority motivated his reply to a letter from the famed British historian Lord Acton, who had asked his views on southern and national affairs. Lee said that southerners accepted in good faith the results of the Civil War, including the elimination of slavery. He expressed the belief that the constitutional power of the Federal government was the source of the nation's peace and safety at home and abroad.

But he also defended states' rights as an essential part of the organic social contract. Calling upon the recorded objections of George Washington and Thomas Jefferson to national centralization, Lee said, "I consider [the constitutional authority of the states] as the chief source of stability to our political system, whereas the consolidation of the states into one vast republic, sure to be aggressive abroad and despotic at home, will be the certain precursor of that ruin which has overwhelmed all those that have preceded it." That Lee's postwar fears of the dangers of national consolidation were exaggerated would in time become evident. That in the midst of the fierce emotions and ominous rhetoric of the Reconstruction period he was sincere in expressing them is equally clear.

In his letter to Lord Acton and in other correspondence Lee explained secession as having been a defense of states' rights rather than of slavery. Because prior to the war he had not been an extreme advocate of states' rights, his biographer Freeman attributed his postwar attitude to his associations during the conflict.

Modern critics of Lee reductively explain his postwar view as being a mere rationalization of southern motives. To a point, this doubtless was the case; every postwar society tends to exalt its motives for having gone to war. Both southerners and northerners did so. Southerners said they did not go to war in order to preserve slavery; northerners said they went to war in order to abolish slavery. Both claims were partly true, partly false.

But the political doctrine of states' rights had a long history. It had been invoked with no connection to slavery by such distinguished Virginians as George Mason and James Madison, as well as by Jefferson, and also by many notable nonsoutherners. Certainly, it was of itself a revered principle in the minds of most southern leaders, so much so, ironically, that it was a significant source of opposition to the efforts of the Confederacy to mobilize southern resources for the prosecution of the war. During and after the war Lee was heavily exposed to the states' rights arguments of his associates. Very probably he was influenced by them, as Freeman said he was.

That Lee was accurate in saying that southerners had not fought for the purpose of preserving slavery is supported by the letters

Confederate soldiers wrote from the battlefield. The vast majority of the soldiers said they fought to defend such noble ideals as liberty or independence, or to protect their homes and families. There is no reason to doubt the sincerity of these statements. The problem in sorting out southern motives for going to war is that in the context of the times a southern defense of states' rights or anything else involved a defense of slavery too.

Lee's fullest public affirmation of sentiment on the question of the creation of the Reconstruction state governments and of black suffrage appeared in a statement prepared by a Virginia lawyer and signed by Lee and various other influential southerners. It opposed the placing of the political power of a state in the hands of the blacks. It denied any feeling of enmity toward them but repeated Lee's earlier conviction that at the time they lacked the intelligence and other qualifications for exercising such power.

Privately, Lee expressed himself more vehemently on the situation created by the Reconstruction acts. He felt that the passage of these acts was a repudiation of the terms on which the South had surrendered. He deplored what he said was the destruction of the Constitution and the freedom of the people. He said he grieved for posterity, American principles, and American liberty, and that the nation's boasted self-government was becoming the jeer and laughingstock of the world.

Privately also, he advised a relative who was attempting to start a farm to hire white laborers only, saying that the presence of blacks always caused a deterioration of conditions, while the presence of whites brought improvement. The key to this particular judgment was his belief, as expressed to another person, that the blacks were plotting against their employers. Just what he meant by this is not clear. Apparently he had in mind the blacks' collaboration with Republican agents who were wooing them with promises that southern lands would be confiscated and divided among them.

He immediately softened his severe judgment of the blacks by saying that he wished them no harm and would do everything in his power to help them. He said he realized they were being misled by persons in their confidence. But, he continued, "our material, social and political interests are naturally with the whites."

There were, admittedly, ambivalences in Lee's attitudes toward blacks as laborers. Later he wrote to a northern man agreeing with the man's sentiments that southerners ought to be the ones to solve the region's racial problems, that the blacks in his vicinity were content, that they had plenty of opportunities for employment, and that their employers held kind feelings toward them. Several months had elapsed since he uttered his previous warnings. Possibly, after observing the conditions in his area, Lee had second thoughts on the matter.

Despite Lee's sharp private expressions of condemnation of the Reconstruction governments, he exercised admirable discretion in his actions and public statements throughout the few remaining years of his life. Although he opposed the immediate enfranchisement of the ex-slaves, he never indicated a belief in their permanent disfranchisement, or in their inherent lack of sufficient intelligence to participate in the political process. Instead, in explaining his views before Congress, he said, "What the future may prove, how intelligent they [the blacks] may become, with what eyes they may look upon the interests of the state in which they reside, I cannot say."

Asked by the congressional committee how he felt about the education of blacks, he replied obliquely, saying that those persons with whom he was associated believed that both races would be benefited if the blacks should be educated. Asked pointedly whether he believed blacks were as capable as whites of acquiring knowledge, he expressed the opinion that they were not, but he added that some were more apt than others. He also protested that he was not particularly qualified to answer such questions.

Lee's views on conditions in the South were not inflexible. Shortly after the war he wrote to General Beauregard, explaining philosophically his attitude toward the state of affairs arising out of Confederate defeat, saying, "I need not tell you that true patriotism sometimes requires of men to act exactly contrary, at one period, to that which it does at another, and the motive which impels them—the desire to do right—is precisely the same. The circumstances which govern their actions, change, and their conduct must conform to the new order of things." Significantly, Beauregard later would lead a political movement of white and black cooperation in Louisiana. There is no evidence that Lee directly influenced him to undertake this plan. But certainly, the Louisianan was indirectly affected by Lee's general outlook on the political affairs of the South.

When it became apparent that the ex-slaves were to be enfranchised, Lee accepted the outcome and advised those whites who were permitted to vote and hold office (many whites were themselves disfranchised at the moment) to do so, and he urged the voters to support the best candidates available, by which he doubtless meant Democrats. He also urged these candidates, if elected, to serve in the new regime in order to exercise their influence on its policies. As he expected, however, the southern state governments that soon emerged were controlled by a Republican coalition of blacks, northern migrants who were known contemptuously to the majority of white southerners as "carpetbaggers," and southern whites who joined the Republicans and were given the epithet "scalawags."

An analysis of the quality of these state governments is beyond the scope of the present study. They portended a complete political, economic, and social revolution within the region; they were viewed by most southern whites, and later by many nonsoutherners, as being grossly incompetent, extravagant, and corrupt, a judgment that has been moderated, but not altogether overturned, by twentieth-century scholarship. To Lee, the state of affairs that emerged in the South seemed to confirm his prediction that the blacks would be misled by demagogues.

Unquestionably, Beauregard and many other southerners were guided by Lee's behavior and advice opposing violence against the ex-slaves or their political allies. A letter from one of Lee's former officers from Mississippi gives a hint of Lee's influence in the postwar South: "Your great and wise example of retirement and peace, obedience to government and law we are all pursuing and following. . . . All your old men here are peacefully at work trying to build up their shattered fortunes, and the Country, its peace and prosperity."

Many southerners did not share the Mississippian's views. The region seethed with wrath over the new state of affairs; the Ku Klux Klan and other bands devoted to violence began to spring up. There is no credible evidence that Lee ever belonged to, encouraged, or endorsed such groups. In his known correspondence on the subject of the Reconstruction acts and the state governments created as a result of them, he advised legal and peaceful measures of recourse, and patience to allow time for "reason and charity to resume their sway."

Many prominent southerners who initially joined the Klan soon began to drop out of it. The year before Lee's death the head of the Klan, the redoubtable former cavalryman Forrest, formally dissolved the notorious organization. Lee had no direct part in the dissolution of the Klan. Various factors, including the threat of Federal reprisals, influenced the decision. But Lee's advice and example had a powerful hidden effect. The dissolution of the Klan did not end the violence; after Lee's death it increased in intensity. Unacceptable as many of his views are today, he provided an indispensable model of decorum and restraint amid the stormy passions of his own era.

However upset he might have been over the affairs of the

South, Lee remained true to his nature in continuing to affirm hope to fellow southerners. On one occasion he said, "The dominant party cannot reign forever, and truth and justice will at last prevail." Later, in a more general and metaphysical observation, he wrote: "My experience of men has neither disposed me to think worse of them nor indisposed me to serve them; nor, in spite of failures which I lament, of errors which I now see and acknowledge, or the present aspect of affairs, do I despair of the future. The truth is this: The march of Providence is so slow and our desires so impatient; the work of progress so immense and our means of aiding it so feeble; the life of humanity is so long, that of the individual so brief, that we often see only the ebb of the advancing wave and are thus discouraged. It is history that teaches us to hope."

Lee retained his equanimity over his own losses and those of his family that resulted from his having served the Confederacy. He continued to cherish the hope that Arlington would one day be restored to his wife, or to their son Custis. When Congress in 1869 refused to permit the return of the George Washington relics that had been confiscated by Union forces at Arlington, Lee wrote that he hoped the presence of these articles in the nation's capital would help to keep alive the memory of the great patriot's principles and virtues. Of the many individuals holding items that had been looted from Arlington, Lee said: "I hope the possessors appreciate them and may imitate the example of their original owner, whose conduct must at times be brought to their recollection by these silent monitors. In this way, they will accomplish good to the country."

His unhappiest personal relationships with blacks, Federal officials, and resentful elements of the northern population grew out of his connection with the college. In the winter of 1867 some of his students were involved in a fracas with a group of blacks, with the result that Lee expelled one of the students and reprimanded the others. A year later he was obliged to demand the withdrawal of two students who had joined with a number of townspeople in chasing a former Union soldier away from skating on a nearby river. Both of these episodes caused investigations to be made by Federal occupation officials, who in both cases fully approved of Lee's actions. The altercation among the skaters had an unfortunate aftermath, however, when a distorted account of it was published in certain northern newspapers in an effort to prevent northern citizens from responding favorably to a request for donations to support the college. In dealing with these disturbances, Lee conducted himself with absolute fairness and propriety, yet he was grieved by them, for he felt that they kept alive the embers of sectional animosity. In spite of such occurrences, the college did receive generous donations from a number of northern philanthropists.

In May 1869 Lee met once again the man who had vanquished him in the field, now President U. S. Grant. Lee had received word that Grant would welcome him to his office in Washington. Whether Grant intended this as an opportunity to discuss southern affairs or simply as an act of courtesy between honorable soldiers is indeterminable. No record of the conversation remains. Lee appeared quite reserved. When he explained that he had been in Baltimore on the business of a prospective railroad, Grant apparently sought to stir the atmosphere with a bit of humor, albeit of the grim sort, by saying, "You and I, general, have had more to do with destroying railroads than with building them." Lee did not respond, but turned to another and presumably more pleasant topic. After about fifteen minutes of conversation the two men who had played cardinal roles in the immense tragic drama of the Civil War parted, to meet no more.

Lee's remaining years were rich in his private life as well as in his professional endeavors. Although his wife was now a complete invalid, confined largely to her bed or chair, he lived contentedly with her and their three surviving daughters. His care for Mrs. Lee's well-being and comfort was a source of admiration among all of their acquaintances. The Lees occasionally journeyed to the famous resort springs in West Virginia, where he renewed his ties with old friends and paid innocent gallantries to the bevies of young women who often gathered about him. He showed an easy and unfeigned courtesy to all, including strangers and northerners who came that way.

Wherever Lee went in the South, his fame was manifest. In Petersburg in the autumn of 1867 for his son Rooney's wedding, Lee found his way lined with cheering citizens. Virginia mountaineers selling their produce at the White Sulphur Springs recognized their old commander and immediately gave him their most stirring tribute, the Rebel Yell. His visit to Baltimore was greeted with attention and applause. On the most extensive trip he made after the war, a journey with his daughter Agnes in the spring of 1870 to the grave of his daughter Annie in North Carolina and to that of his father on Cumberland Island off the Georgia coast, then south to Florida and back to Savannah and Charleston, he was honored repeatedly with massive ovations or reverential silences and bared heads.

Except for occasional flare-ups of anger and resentment over what he considered the mistreatment of the South, Lee remained faithful to the two most powerful influences of his life: religion and the code of the gentleman. In his mind the two were inseparable: both demanded courage, obedience to duty, kindness, humility, and subjection to the divine will. He summed up his own concept of the gentleman in these lines: "The forbearing use of power does not only form a touchstone, but the manner in which an individual enjoys certain advantages over others is a test of a true gentleman. . . . A true man of honor feels humbled himself when he cannot help humbling others." He expressed the essence of his religious belief, undoubtedly strengthened by his own experience in life, when he told a young mother who asked a blessing on her child, "Teach him he must deny himself."

Lee's once-splendid physique declined rapidly after the war; the responsibilities of command and the trauma of defeat had taken a heavy toll on his vitality. A photograph of him at age sixty-three displayed a countenance full of character and grace, but it revealed the face of an ancient.

Lee fell ill in the fall of 1869 of what proved to be a heart malady, probably angina pectoris. His condition soon improved to the point that he was able to continue his presidential duties throughout the winter of the 1869–70 school year. In the spring, before the close of the term, he took the long trip south, which, though tiring and carried out in constant chest pain, left him feeling somewhat stronger than before.

He opened the college session on September 15 and for two weeks conducted the school's affairs as usual. On the twenty-eighth he spent the day in routine administrative duties, and from four o'clock in the afternoon until past seven he presided over a meeting of the Episcopal church vestry, on which he had served since coming to Lexington. The time was nearing eight when he stood before his dinner table at home to ask the blessing. He opened his mouth but no words came. He then sank exhausted into his chair but still could make no reply to his wife's worried suggestion that he take a cup of tea. Instead, a look of resignation came into his eyes, and he deliberately drew himself upright in his seat, a soldier to the end.

For more than two weeks Lee lived and at times appeared to rally. Physicians ministered solicitously to him, and his family and friends, including one of his professors, Colonel William Preston Johnston, son of Albert Sidney, kept an anxious vigil at his bedside. Lee dutifully swallowed the prescribed medicines when they were administered by the physicians, though eventually he began to refuse them from his family and once told his daughter Agnes that all was useless.

The morning of October 10 he said haltingly, "I feel better." Suddenly during the afternoon he began to fail, and throughout the night he grew progressively weaker. The following morning he became half delirious. He seemed transported back into battle, perhaps to the moment of crisis at the end of the day at Antietam. Professor Johnston remembered his saying, "Tell Hill he must come up."*

Throughout the day and night of the eleventh, Lee lingered. At 9:30 the following morning he died.

---

* Exactly what Lee said, if anything, as he approached the end cannot be determined with certainty. Johnston recorded also that shortly before his death Lee said, "Strike the tent." The physicians who attended Lee did not indicate in their report either of the utterances quoted by Johnston. Two present-day physicians who have examined the accounts of Lee's final illness and death have questioned his having said them. These physicians believe he died of a paralytic stroke that probably made speech impossible at that time. On the other hand, Mrs. Lee, writing a few weeks after his death, said of his last hours, "His mind wandered to those dreadful battlefields."

Epilogue

Two figures tower above all others in the national mythology surrounding the Civil War: Abraham Lincoln and Robert E. Lee. Lincoln won the war with grace, preserved the Union, emancipated the slaves, welcomed the defeated South back to its national allegiance with the words "With malice toward none; with charity for all," and at war's end requested the playing of the Confederate national anthem, "Dixie," which he said he had always been fond of. Lee lost the war with grace, affirmed the magnanimity of his victorious adversary, urged his fellow southerners to accept the verdict of the battlefield and resume their roles as American citizens, rejected wealth and ease for himself, and devoted his remaining years and powerful influence to serving the youth of the South and healing the wounds of war.

Near the End of Life

Selected Readings

The complete bibliography covering Lee's career is immense. In addition to the numerous works that are specifically addressed to his life, a significant proportion of the many thousands of other writings on the Civil War deal to some extent with his military leadership. General books on the war are omitted from the present selections, which comprise only a list of the works most useful in the preparation of this volume.

Any study of Lee's career must depend heavily on three sets of books: *The War of the Rebellion: A Compilation of the Official Records of the Union and Confederate Armies,* 128 vols. and index (Washington, D.C.: Government Printing Office, 1880–1901), which is the great primary source on the military operations of the Civil War; and Douglas Southall Freeman, *R. E. Lee: A Biography,* 4 vols. (New York, London: Charles Scribner's Sons, 1934–42), and its supplement, *Lee's Lieutenants: A Study in Command,* 3 vols. (New York: Charles Scribner's Sons, 1942–44). Freeman's works on Lee, hailed initially as being definitive, have in recent years been sharply criticized as being too reverential toward their subject. Notwithstanding this tendency, they remain the greatest source of organized and evaluated information on his life. The majority of Freeman's conclusions have stood the test of time and scholarship.

Among the early, eulogistic studies of Lee are James D. McCabe, Jr., *Life and Campaigns of General Robert E. Lee* (New York and New Orleans: Blelock & Co., 1867); "A Distinguished Southern Journalist" [Edward A. Pollard], *The Early Life, Campaigns, and Public Service of Robert E. Lee* (New York: E. B. Treat & Co., Publishers, 1870); John Esten Cooke, *A Life of Gen. Robert E. Lee* (New York: D. Appleton and Company, 1871); Armistead L. Long, *Memoirs of Robert E. Lee: His Military and Personal History* (New York, Philadelphia, and Washington, D.C.: J. M. Stoddart & Company, 1886); J. William Jones, *Personal Reminiscences, Ancedotes and Letters of Gen. Robert E. Lee* (New York: D. Appleton and Company, 1874); and *The Life and Letters of Robert Edward Lee: Soldier and Man* (New York and Washington, D.C.: Neale Publishing Company, 1906). Robert E. Lee, Jr., *Recollections of General Robert E. Lee* (New York: Doubleday, Page & Company, 1904), is useful. The most engaging of all eulogistic biographies of Lee is Thomas Nelson Page, *Robert E. Lee: Man and Soldier* (New York: Charles Scribner's Sons, 1911).

Laudatory works by foreign authors include Frederic Maurice, *Robert E. Lee the Soldier* (Boston and New York: Houghton Mifflin Company, 1925); G. F. R. Henderson, *The Science of War: A Collection of Essays and Lectures* (London, New York, and Bombay: Longmans, Green, and Co., 1905); Garnet J. Wolseley, *General Lee* (Rochester, N.Y.: Press of C. Mann Printing Company, 1906); Cyril Falls, *A Hundred Years of War* (London: Duckworth, 1953); and F. E. Adcock, *The Greek and Macedonian Art of War* (Berkeley: University of California Press, 1957).

Admiring books that emphasize Lee as a national figure are Gamaliel Bradford, *Lee the American* (Boston: Houghton Mifflin

Company, 1927); and Marshall W. Fishwick, *Lee after the War* (New York: Dodd, Mead & Company, 1963).

More recent works that are strongly sympathetic to Lee are Margaret Sanborn, *Robert E. Lee: A Portrait* and *Robert E. Lee: The Complete Man* (Philadelphia and New York: J. B. Lippincott Company, 1966, 1967); and Charles Bracelen Flood, *Lee: The Last Years* (Boston: Houghton Mifflin Company, 1981). Favorable assessments of Lee's military leadership occur in Richard M. McMurry, *Two Great Rebel Armies: An Essay in Confederate Military History* (Chapel Hill: University of North Carolina Press, 1989); Charles P. Roland, "The Generalship of Robert E. Lee," in *Grant, Lee, Lincoln and the Radicals: Essays on Civil War Leadership,* ed. by Grady McWhiney (Evanston, Ill.: Northwestern University Press, 1964); and Gary W. Gallagher, "'Upon Their Success Hang Momentous Interests': Generals," in *Why the Confederacy Lost,* ed. by Gabor S. Boritt (New York and Oxford: Oxford University Press, 1992).

A landmark critical work on Lee published prior to World War II is J. F. C. Fuller, *Grant and Lee: A Study in Personality and Generalship* (New York: Charles Scribner's Sons, 1933), which questions Lee's logistical abilities, command decisions, and strategic thinking. Early studies criticizing Lee for an excessive tendency to launch attacks are the British military historian B. H. Liddell Hart, "Lee: A Psychological Problem," *Saturday Review of Literature,* XI (December 15, 1934), and "Why Lee Lost Gettysburg," *ibid.* (March 23, 1935).

Among the critical studies of Lee's military leadership published since World War II are T. Harry Williams, "Freeman: Historian of the Civil War: An Appraisal," *Journal of Southern History,* XXI (February, 1955), and "The Military Leadership of North and South," in *Why the North Won the Civil War,* ed. by David Donald (Baton Rouge: Louisiana State University Press, 1960); Archer Jones, *Confederate Strategy from Shiloh to Vicksburg*

(Baton Rouge: Louisiana State University Press, 1961); Herman Hattaway and Archer Jones, *How the North Won: A Military History of the Civil War* (Urbana, Chicago, and London: University of Illinois Press, 1983); Grady McWhiney and Perry D. Jamieson, *Attack and Die: Civil War Military Tactics and the Southern Heritage* (Tuscaloosa, Ala.: University of Alabama Press, 1982); Richard E. Beringer, Herman Hattaway, Archer Jones, and William N. Still, *Why the South Lost the Civil War* (Athens, Ga.: University of Georgia Press, 1986); and Thomas Lawrence Connelly and Archer Jones, *The Politics of Command: Factions and Ideas in Confederate Strategy* (Baton Rouge: Louisiana State University Press, 1973).

Archer Jones, *Civil War Command and Strategy: The Process of Victory and Defeat* (New York, Toronto, Oxford, Singapore, and Sydney: The Free Press, 1992), criticizes Lee's strategic decisions but praises him as an army commander. Jones, "Military Means, Political Ends: Strategy," in Boritt, *Why the Confederacy Lost,* offers a judicious evaluation of Lee's generalship. Gary W. Gallagher, ed., *The Third Day at Gettysburg & Beyond* (Chapel Hill and London: University of North Carolina Press, 1994), is a volume of thoughtful essays on the facts and myths surrounding Lee's fatal decision to deliver the Confederate attack on the final day at Gettysburg.

Works that disparage Lee the man as well as Lee the soldier include Liddell Hart, "Lee: A Psychological Problem"; Thomas L. Connelly, *The Marble Man: Robert E. Lee and His Image in American Society* (New York: Alfred A. Knopf, 1977); and Alan T. Nolan, *Lee Considered: General Robert E. Lee and Civil War History* (Chapel Hill and London: University of North Carolina Press, 1991). Liddell Hart offers the paradoxical opinion that Lee's high standing as a cadet and his steadiness of character merely guaranteed him a prospect of "admirable mediocrity" in his career. Connelly presents a psychobiographical study alleging that Lee's obsession with his father's derelictions and excesses, his (Robert E. Lee's) lack of a satisfying marital relationship, and his conviction of failure in life created weaknesses in his own character and personality, and, in turn, in his generalship. Nolan expounds an argument previously set forth by Liddell Hart, Connelly, and McWhiney and Jamieson that a compulsion for offensive warfare doomed Lee to defeat. Nolan also employs presentist judgments and prosecutorial methods to indict Lee's character and motives.

Index